The Economic Implications of

# Climate
# Change

in Britain

The Economic Implications of

# Climate Change

in Britain

Edited by Martin Parry and Rachel Duncan

**Earthscan Publications Ltd, London**

First published in 1995 by
Earthscan Publications Limited
120 Pentonville Road, London N1 9JN

A catalogue record for this book is available from the British Library

ISBN: 1 85383 240 5

Typesetting and figures by PCS Mapping & DTP, Newcastle upon Tyne
    and Drawing Office, UCL Department of Geography
Printed and bound in Great Britain by Biddles Ltd, Guildford
    and Kings Lynn

Earthscan Publications Limited is an editorially independent subsidiary
of Kogan Page Limited and publishes in association with the
International Institute for Environment and Development and WWF-UK.

# Contents

# Foreword

In February 1994, the Green College Centre for Environmental Policy and Understanding was the host for a seminar on the Economic Implications of Climate Change in Britain, together with Martin Parry, then Director of the Environmental Change Unit at the University of Oxford and now Director of the Jackson Environment Institute and the Environmental Studies Programme at University College London. The purpose of this meeting was to take stock, two years after the Rio Summit and one year before the First Conference of the Parties to the UN Framework Convention on Climate Change, of our knowledge of the potential impacts of climate change. There were seventy seminar participants drawn from universities, industry and government. Papers were presented on best estimates of future climate change for Britain, and their likely impact on agriculture, ecosystems, water resources, coastal regions, energy, and the finance and insurance sectors. In each instance, speakers were paired in such a way that those experts concerned with the biophysical aspects of effects were brought together with those more concerned with their economic and social implications. The meeting was thus as much an opportunity for a meeting of minds amongst the speakers as for communication between speakers and audience. The results of this dialogue are to be seen in this book: the chapters represent an attempt to bridge the physical, economic and social aspects of the implications of climate change. In this sense they represent an advance on the first report of the Climate Change Impacts Review Group of the British Department of the Environment (1991).

This book goes to press as the First Conference of the Parties to the UN Framework Convention on Climate Change meets in Berlin. The purpose of this Conference is to agree upon the next steps to be taken towards achieving the Convention's ultimate objective: 'to achieve stabilization of greenhouse gas concentrations in the atmosphere at a level that would prevent dangerous anthropogenic interference with the climate system'. The book is an example of the regional scientific assessment that is needed to distinguish between dangerous magnitudes or rates of climate change and those that can be adapted to by ecosystems and do not threaten the security of food production or the sustainability of economic development. More studies of this kind are needed, particularly in those regions (such as the semi-arid tropics) which are inherently vulnerable to climatic variability today, in order to provide a solid scientific basis upon which international negotiations can move forward.

*Crispin Tickell*
*Green College Centre for Environmental Policy and Understanding*

# Preface

This book brings together a series of papers written by experts on the potential effects of climate change in Britain. All 17 authors are active researchers in this field, four of them are senior authors of the Intergovernmental Panel on Climate Change and three are members of the UK Department of Environment's Climate Change Impacts Review Group.

Much of the assessments to date of the effects of climate change have concentrated on impacts on physical resources and landscape. This is true of estimated effects for Britain, for Europe and for impacts worldwide. Thus, while little attention has been paid to the economic implications of changes in resource availability due to climate change, these may be the most important effects for humankind.

For this reason, this collection of papers seeks a balance between the estimation of the effects on physical resources and the evaluation of implications for resource use. Inevitably assumptions are made about effects outside Britain and their consequences for Britain itself. In many cases – for example, in the case of food availability and food prices – the worldwide effects of climate change working through the world food trade system and finally affecting Britain, may be more important than the effects of climate changes occurring over Britain itself. These and many other implications remain to be explored in much more detail.

The editors and authors acknowledge the support of Nuclear Electric plc; the Centre for Social and Economic Research on the Global Environment (CSERGE); the Water Directorate of the Department of the Environment, (DoE contract PECD/7/7/348); the Chartered Insurance Institute, for permitting the use of edited parts of their report *The Impact of Changing Weather Patterns on Property Insurance*; and also Megan Gawith for her assistance in the section on subsidence. Thanks to David Pearce and Andrew Sample for their helpful comments on Chapter 3; to the Ministry of Agriculture, Fisheries and Food and the Economic and Social Research Council; research on agriculture, reported in Chapter 4 was conducted in collaboration with M D A Rounsevell (Soil Survey and Land Research Centre, Cranfield University); Jianmin Shao (Vaisala TMI Ltd); Philip Jones, Richard Tranter and John Marsh (Centre for Agricultural Strategy, University of Reading); and Tahir Rehman (Department of Agriculture, University of Reading).

*Martin Parry, Jackson Environment Institute, University College London*
*Rachel Duncan, Green College Centre for Environmental Policy and*
*Understanding*
*February 1995*

# Contributors

**Nigel Arnell** Reader in Physical Geography, Department of Geography, University of Southampton, Highfield, Southampton SO17 1BJ (*Chapter 3*)

**Paul Brignall** Research Associate, Environmental Change Unit, University of Oxford, 1a Mansfield Road, Oxford OX1 3TB (*Chapter 4*)

**Alun Davies** Acclimatory Physiology Department, AFRC Institute of Grassland and Environmental Research, Plas Gogerddan, Aberystwyth, Dyfed SY23 3EB (*Chapter 4*)

**Andrew Dlugolecki** Chief Manager, UK Operations, General Accident Fire and Life Assurance Corporation, Pithcavlis, Perth, Scotland PH2 0NH (*Chapter 6*)

**Richard Dubourg** Research Associate, Centre for Social and Economic Research on the Global Environment (CSERGE), University College London, Gower Street, London, WC1E 6BT (*Chapter 3*)

**Rachel Duncan** Research Officer, Green College Centre for Environmental Policy and Understanding, Green College, at the Radcliffe Observatory, Oxford OX2 6HG (01865 311038) (*Editor*)

**Samuel Fankhauser** Research Associate, Centre for Social and Economic Research on the Global Environment (CSERGE), University College London and University of East Anglia, Gower St, London WC1E 6BT (*Chapter 7*)

**Paula Harrison** Research Associate, Environmental Change Unit, University of Oxford, 1a Mansfield Road, Oxford, OX1 3TB (*Chapter 6*)

**Chris Hope** Lecturer, Judge Institute of Management Studies, University of Cambridge, Mill Lane, Cambridge CB2 1RX (*Chapter 7*)

**Jo Hossell** Research Associate, Environmental Change Unit, University of Oxford, 1a Mansfield Road, Oxford OX1 3TB (*Chapter 4*)

**Jeremy Leggett** Director, Science, Atmosphere and Energy Campaign, Greenpeace International, Greenpeace, Canonbury Villas, London N1 2PN (*Chapter 6*)

**Jean Palutikof** Assistant Director (Research), Climatic Research Unit, University of East Anglia, Norwich, Norfolk NR4 7TJ (*Chapter 6*)

**Martin Parry** Director, Jackson Environment Institute and Professor of Environmental Management, University College London, 26 Bedford Way, London WC1H OAP (0171 380 7577) (*Editor, Chapter 1, Chapter 4*)

**Chris Pollock** Director, AFRC Institute of Grassland and Environmental Research, Plas Gogerddan, Aberystwyth, Dyfed SY23 3EB (*Chapter 4*)

**Jim Skea** British Gas/ESRC Professorial Fellow, Programme on Environmental Policy and Regulation, Science Policy Research Unit, Mantell Building, University of Sussex, Falmer, Brighton, East Sussex BN1 9RF (*Chapter 5*)

**Michael Tooley** Professor, Department of Geography and the Environmental Research Centre, University of Durham, Science Laboratories, Durham DH1 3LE (*Chapter 2*)

**Kerry Turner** Executive Director, Centre for Social and Economic Research on the Global Environment (CSERGE), University of East Anglia, Norwich, Norfolk NR4 7TJ (*Chapter 2*)

# Abbreviations

| | |
|---|---|
| BP | before present |
| CBA | cost benefit analysis |
| CCGT | combined cycle gas turbine |
| CCIRG | climate Change Impacts Review Group |
| CFC | chlorofluorocarbon |
| CLUAM | climate land use allocation model |
| $CO_2$ | carbon dioxide |
| CSIRO | Commonwealth Scientific Institute and Research Organisation |
| CZMS | Coastal Zone Management Study |
| DICE | Dynamic Integrated Climate Economy – model |
| ENSO | El Niño southern oscillation |
| GCM | general circulation model |
| GFDL | Geophysical Fluid Dynamics Laboratory |
| GISS | Goddard Institute for Space Studies |
| GNP | gross national product |
| HCFC | hydrochlorofluorocarbon |
| IGCC | integrated gasification combined cycle |
| IPCC | Intergovernmental Panel on Climate Change |
| MINK | Missouri, Iowa, Nebraska and Kansas – impact case study |
| NFFO | non-fossil fuel obligation |
| NRA | National Rivers Authority |
| OD | Ordnance Datum |
| OECD | Organisation for Economic Co-operation and Development |
| OFWAT | Office of Water Services |
| PAGE | Policy Analysis of the Greenhouse Effect – model |
| PWR | pressurised water reactor |
| RQO | river quality objective |
| SWQO | statutory water quality objective |
| UKMO | United Kingdom Meteorological Office |
| UKTR | United Kingdom Transient Response |

# List of Illustrations

## Figures

# Tables

# 1

# Background to Possible Changes in the British Climate

The purpose of the chapters that follow is to consider what effects might occur in Britain as a result of a range of possible future changes in climate. At the outset it is therefore useful to specify this range so that the chapters assess broadly similar situations and so that a sector-to-sector comparison of impacts may be made. This background note therefore provides a brief statement of current state-of-the-art scenarios (or internally consistent pictures) of climate change that relate to Britain.

As a result largely of human activities, particularly of the burning of fossil fuels and deforestation, the concentration of so-called 'greenhouse gases' in the atmosphere has been increasing. Carbon dioxide has increased by a quarter above pre-industrial levels and methane has doubled. These gases, and others such as nitrous oxide, have the property of changing the heat budget of the atmosphere such that the Earth's surface and lower atmosphere should warm as their concentration increases.

There are many uncertainties. Rates of concentration increases will vary according to rates of emission and the latter are very much affected by variations in energy use, types of fuel used and, of course, by population size and its level of affluence. The sensitivity of the climate to different levels of greenhouse gas concentration is unclear, and the regional pattern of a change in climate forced by greenhouse gases is unknown. These uncertainties were spelled out in the First Assessment Report of the Intergovernmental Panel on Climate Change (IPCC) (IPCC 1990). At that time the judgement was that average global surface temperatures could increase by between 1.5°C and 4.5°C as a result of greenhouse gas, equivalent to a doubling of atmospheric carbon dioxide. This climate response might be expected to occur in c2060 under best-guess projections of future emissions inferred from, for example, United Nations best estimates of population growth, future affluence levels, and developments in technology (IPCC 1990). Using the IPCC socio-economic scenarios the UK Climate

*1*

Change Impacts Review Group estimated global average temperatures would be 0.7°C, 1.4°C and 2.1°C higher than today in years 2010, 2030 and 2050 respectively (CCIRG 1991). Subsequently a supplement to the first IPCC report, which referred to the 'business as usual' scenario as IS92a, confirmed the original figures to 1.5≈4.5°C (IPCC 1992). The IPCC's Second Assessment Report will be published in 1996.

Whatever the estimate of response by the global climate, the regional picture, at least at the level of resolution to enable us to map the climate of Britain (say, down to the 50km square), remains elusive. As a result it would be wise not to pin a set of assessments on one scenario alone, even if it were the best estimate. For this reason the chapters in this book follow an approach that is more akin to a sensitivity analysis, taking a range of 'not impossible' future climates and asking: what would be their effects on Britain.

This approach still needs to be based upon existing knowledge of the probability of occurrence of different futures, much of which is still limited to a single best estimate. The summary which follows represents our current best knowledge but will almost certainly be improved upon soon.

## The CCIRG 1991 Scenarios

These were derived from IPCC socio-economic scenarios using a simple climate model to provide a transient or time-dependent picture of the possible climate response to greenhouse gas forcing and the average of five general circulation models being used to acquire the spatial pattern of the response models (CCIRG 1991, Wigley and Raper 1992). For the summer season (June, July and August) across the whole of Britain the temperature is estimated to be 0.7°C, 1.4°C and 2.1°C higher for the years 2010, 2030 and 2050 respectively. For the winter season (December, January and February) warming is expected to be greater in the north, with the estimates of increase being 0.7°C (southern Britain) to 1.6°C (northern Britain) for 2010, 1.4°C to 3.2°C for 2030, and 2.1°C to 4.7°C for 2050. The CCIRG scenario indicates no clear change in summer rainfall, and increased winter precipitation of 3 ± 3 per cent, 5 ± 5 per cent and 8 ± 8 per cent for 2010, 2030 and 2050.

## The UK Transient Scenarios (UKTR)

More recent transient experiments with general circulation models, such as those with the UK High Resolution model, have enabled the spatial pattern of the climate response to be simulated more accurately (Hadley Centre 1992). There is indicated for the British Isles in Figures 1.1 and 1.2. They suggest increases of 1°C to 2°C in summer and winter, with perhaps greater rates of increase in the east than the west. Winter precipitation is expected to increase, particularly in the south. Summer rainfall is shown to increase in the north and decrease in the south.

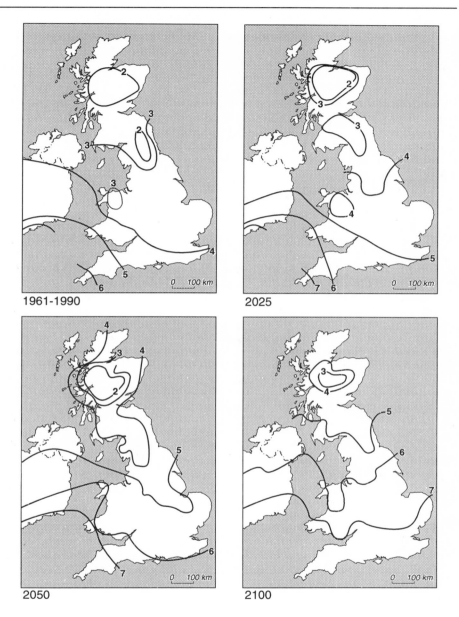

**Figure 1.1** *Mean winter (December, January, February) surface air temperature °C for the UK observed for a) 1961–90 and estimated for b) 2025, c) 2050 and d) 2100*

The estimated scenarios use the 'linked model' method described in the text and are superimposed on the 1961–90 baseline.

Redrawn from Viner and Hulme, 1994

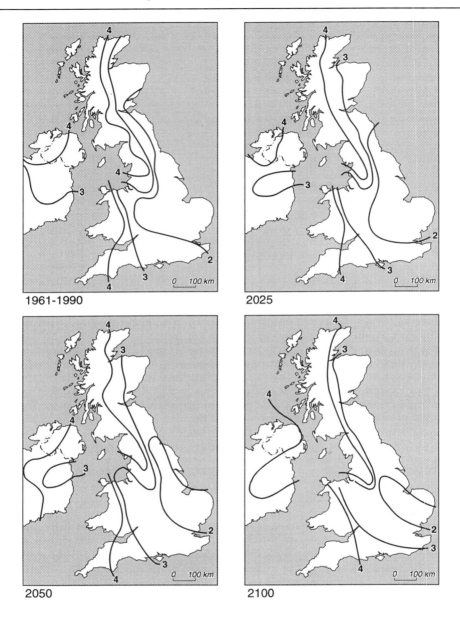

**Figure 1.2** *Mean winter (December, January, February) precipitation mm/day for the UK observed for a) 1961–90 and estimated for b) 2025, c) 2050 and d) 2100*

The estimated scenarios use the 'linked model' method described in the text and are superimposed on the 1961–90 baseline.
Redrawn from Viner and Hulme, 1994

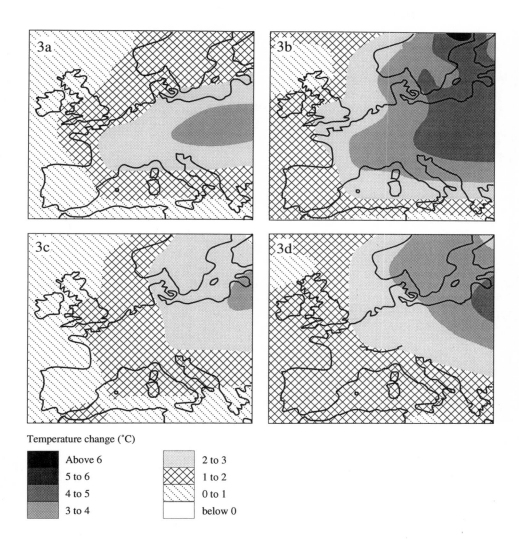

Temperature change (°C)

| | | | |
|---|---|---|---|
| ■ Above 6 | | ▨ 2 to 3 | |
| ■ 5 to 6 | | ▨ 1 to 2 | |
| ■ 4 to 5 | | ▨ 0 to 1 | |
| ▨ 3 to 4 | | □ below 0 | |

**Figure 1.3** *Mean winter (December, January, February) (a and b) and mean summer (June, July, August) (c and d) surface air temperature change for Europe for years 35–44 and 65–74 from the UKTR experiment*

The changes are with respect to the full 75-year control means. Note that the pattern as well as the magnitude of change alters from decade to decade.
Redrawn from Hadley Centre, 1992

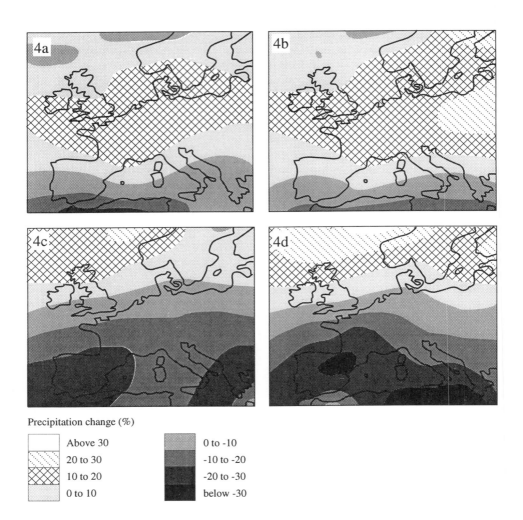

Precipitation change (%)

| | | | |
|---|---|---|---|
| Above 30 | | 0 to -10 | |
| 20 to 30 | | -10 to -20 | |
| 10 to 20 | | -20 to -30 | |
| 0 to 10 | | below -30 | |

**Figure 1.4** *Mean winter (December, January, February) (a and b) and mean summer (June, July, August) (c and d) precipitation change for Europe for years 35–44 and 65–74 from the UKTR experiment*

The changes are with respect to the full 75-year control means. Note that the pattern as well as the magnitude of change alters from decade to decade.
Redrawn from Hadley Centre, 1992

These experiments assume a 1 per cent compound annual increase in greenhouse gas concentrations (which approximates to the IPCC IS92a). But the timing of the response is unclear because of current difficulties in simulating the effect of greenhouse gas emissions on a climate which is assumed to be in equilibrium at the start of the experiment (often taken to be 1985) but

# The LINK scenarios

As a result, the 'linked model' approach used by CCIRG in 1991 but applied to the current general circulation model outputs may represent the preferred approach. Here the simple climate model uses the IPCC best estimates (IS92a) of greenhouse gas concentrations to simulate the global climate response, and the UKTR to provide the spatial pattern for that response (Viner and Hulme 1994).

The estimated changes in climate over the British Isles are given in Figures 1.3 and 1.4. Unlike the preceding figures these do not give difference values (such as increases/decreases in rainfall and temperature), but superimpose the scenario over the actual pattern of current climate which is based on data for the period 1961–90 for a nationwide set of meteorological stations. The figures reveal broadly the same changes as those for the UKTR experiment. They have the advantage of indicating the timing of the changes and the possible resulting changes in the geography of climate in Britain. They have the disadvantage of showing a much greater degree of detail than is justified by the uncertainty of the science. They should be used here merely as a rough guide to what might happen in the future. They are not a forecast of that future.

# 2

# The Effects of Sea-Level Rise

## Introduction

The best-guess global sea-level rise projection for the end of the next century is 48cm (Wigley and Raper 1992). This and earlier projections by the Intergovernmental Panel on Climate Change (IPCC) have become one of the chief criteria for coastal zone management in both the developed and the developing worlds (IPCC 1990, 1992). In Britain, cognisance is given to the IPCC's sea-level rise projections in the design height of sea defences, which in England and Wales alone protect some 700,000ha of agricultural, industrial and residential land below +5.0m OD.[*]

Some of the scientific uncertainties of the sea-level rise projections have been addressed, but others, such as variations in ocean 'topography', have not. In addition, the range of variability of present-day sea level and of sea level during the Recent geological past has not been stressed or clearly understood. Both the individual and the institutional responses depend upon the best information, including uncertainties, communicated simply and effectively.

Some of the uncertainties that have not been addressed in the sea-level rise projections, such as ocean 'topography' or geoidal changes, are considered here, particularly in the way they may affect the coastline of Britain. Attention is drawn to present and past variations in sea level resulting from tidal differences, recent earth movements and variable sediment budgets, all of which affect the measured change of sea level. Stress is placed on the fact that relative sea level can go down as well as up. It is clear that variable rates of sea level have occurred in the past, and that, taken with the delivery of sediment to the coastal zone, this will affect the rate and direction of coastline change. Extreme water levels, such as those caused periodically by astronomical factors, and those caused aperiodically by meteorological processes (for example, storm surges) or submarine geomorphological processes (for exam-

[*] Ordnance Datum, approximately mean sea level at Newlyn, Cornwall

ple, tsunamis: very large waves set off by earthquakes on the ocean bed or continental shelf which rise to greater and greater heights as they approach the coast), have had a profound effect on the coast of Britain.

The extent, nature and history of the coastal lowlands of Britain are summarised as a background to these considerations.

# The Coastal Lowlands of Britain

The distribution of the coastal lowlands of Britain is shown on Figure 2.1. They range in extent from less than a hectare to over 400,000ha in the case of the Fenlands, which is the most extensive coastal lowland in Britain. Their extent was defined by the 25 feet (c7.5m) contour (Tooley 1971) and by the distribution of sediments directly and indirectly influenced by sea level and tidal range. Under storm surge conditions, fresh water from the catchment will back up the river channels, resulting in fresh-water flooding: the landward limit of such flooding is regarded as the effective landward limit of the coastal lowlands, even though the altitude may be greater than +5 or +7.5m OD for some coastal lowlands, but much less for others.

In Britain, as in the Netherlands, the coastal lowlands are divided into tidal flat and lagoonal zones, in which marine sediments have been laid down and a perimarine zone where sedimentation is dominantly under fresh-water conditions (Hageman 1969). Sea-level curves can be constructed from index points derived from dated articulated sequences of marine clays, silts and sands, and locally gravels which are separated by brackish and fresh-water organic deposits, reedswamp and fen peats and locally raised bog peats (Greensmith and Tooley 1982, Shennan et al 1992). Areas in the Fenlands, Teesside coastal lowlands and the south-west Lancashire coastal lowlands are at or below Ordnance Datum. All these areas lie well below the present day high tide levels and are already at risk.

## Present Day Land and Sea-Level Relationships

There is a considerable range of variability of tidal conditions around Britain (Figure 2.2). Adjacent estuaries can display markedly different tidal characteristics, and hence different altitudes at which the spring tide intersects the natural or artificial sea defence. Extreme water levels occur periodically as the result of high astronomical tides, and aperiodically as the result of storm surges and tsunamis. High astronomical tides affecting the coasts of Britain range in altitude from +1.3m OD at Lowestoft to + 8.0m OD at Avonmouth and extreme water levels that have occurred in the past on the east coast of England serve as the basis for calculating the danger-level altitudes as part of the Storm Tide Warning Service. These levels have been exceeded or equalled on 112 occasions for the storm surge seasons 1972–73 to 1988–89 (Coker et al 1989).

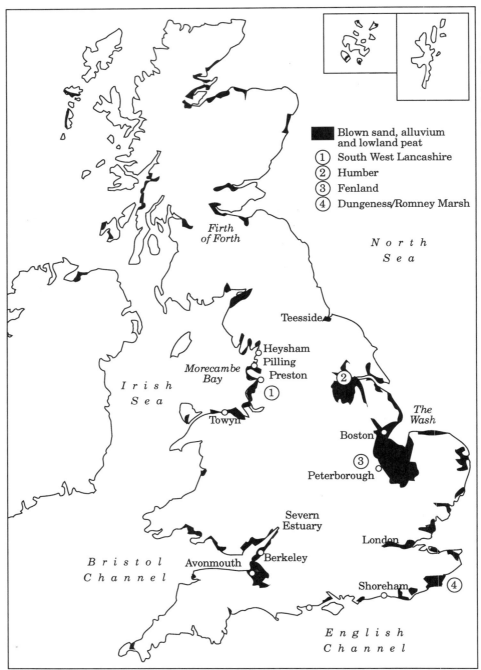

**Figure 2.1** *Map of the UK showing the distribution of blown sand, marine alluvium and lowland peat in the coastal lowlands*

Based on: International Quaternary Map of Europe, Sheet 6 København, 1:2,500,000. Hannover, Germany 1970; Quaternary Map of the United Kingdom, North and South, 1:625,000, Institute of Geological Sciences; and *The Atlas of Britain and Northern Ireland*, p18 superficial deposits, 1:2,000,000.

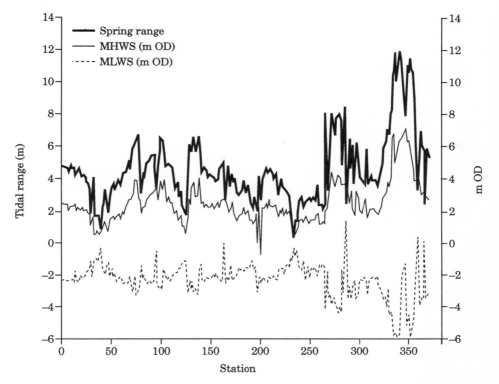

**Figure 2.2** *Mean spring tide ranges and mean high water of spring tides and mean low water of spring tides related to Ordnance Datum (Newlyn) for primary and secondary ports around the coastline of Great Britain*

The station numbers refer to the database of tides in the Environmental Research Centre, Durham. (Admiralty Tide Tables. Reproduced by permission of Dr I. Shennan.) Station 50 is Brading, Isle of Wight; Station 100 is Barnes Bridge, Thames estuary; Station 150 is North Sunderland, Northumberland; Station 200 is Ullapool, north-west Scotland; Station 250 is East Loch Tarbert; Station 300 is Holyhead, Angelsey and Station 350 is Narlwood Rocks, Severn Estuary.
Source: Appendix 1, in Davidson et al 1991

The considerable variation in high tide altitudes and the altitudes of extreme water levels indicates that some coastal lowlands are at greater risk than others. A coastal lowland defined by the +5m OD contour with a mean high water of +1.5m OD, as in the case of Christchurch Harbour, is less vulnerable than a coastal lowland where the mean high water mark of spring tides is +7.2m OD, as in the case of the Severn coastal lowlands at Berkeley. Coastal lowlands will become more at risk if sea level rises, if ground altitudes fall or there is an increase in storminess.

# The Changing Altitudes of the Coastal Lowlands

In general, ground altitudes of the coastal lowlands are less than +5 OD but
the consequences of drainage, sediment dewatering and peat wastage are
that the altitudes are declining, and increasing the area of risk. For example in the Fenlands, south-east of Peterborough, Hutchinson (1980) has
demonstrated that, following the installation of pumps between 1851 and
1962, ground altitudes declined from +1.6m OD to –2.3m OD by 1978
(Figure 2.3). As there are over 2.5m of peat remaining, continued drainage
will result in further ground lowering, eventually to –5m OD. Without natural sea defences, such as sand dunes and shingle banks, and without the
network of maintained artificial defences, such as earth embankments,
some of which are armoured, during the periodic high tides the sea would
penetrate up to 45km landward in the Fenland and water would stand six
metres deep (Tooley 1989).

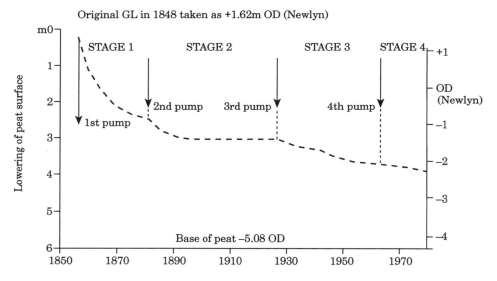

**Figure 2.3** *Lowering of the ground surface at Holme Post, southeast of
Peterborough, in the Fenlands, based on 25 observations made between
1848 and 1978*

GL = Ground Level; OD = Ordnance Datum (Newlyn)
Source: redrawn from Hutchinson (1980)

The coastal lowlands are also affected by long-term earth movements resulting in part from ice loading and delevelling during deglaciation, and in part
from subsidence adjacent to the North Sea sedimentary basin. Both the
rates and directions of movement vary.

Current rates of subsidence (Figure 2.4) in south-east Britain range from
–1mm/year to –1.9mm/year, whereas in central Scotland, uplift rates
approach +2mm/year (Shennan 1989). Longer-term trends indicate up to

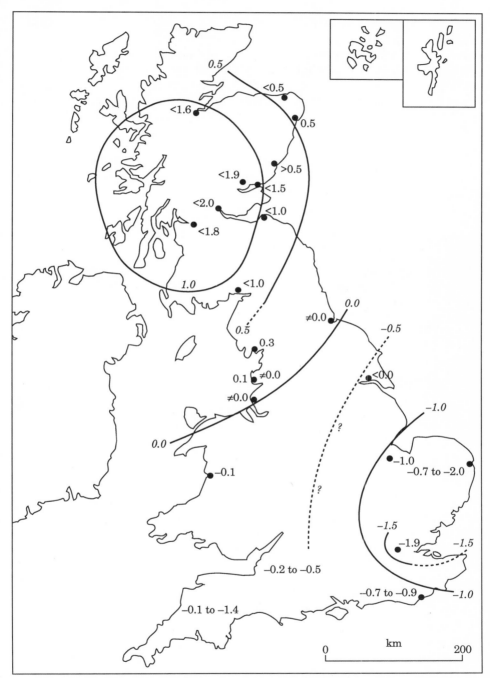

**Figure 2.4** *Map of Great Britain showing estimated current rates of crustal movement (mm/year)*

Source: Shennan 1989

−1.67m/1000 years in south-east Britain, and +1.92m/1000 years in the Firth of Forth (Shennan 1987). Extrapolating these values to 2100 yield values of 15cm subsidence in south-east Britain and 19cm uplift in Scotland. However, simple linear extrapolation fails to accommodate the measured reduction in uplift and subsidence that occurs during an interglacial, and these values will be maximal. The consequences of falling ground altitudes in the coastal lowlands resulting from drainage, and of tectonic subsidence in southeast Britain mean that the relative rise of sea level is already greater than any of the sea-level rise predictions. Any rise of sea level caused by the enhanced greenhouse effect will exacerbate a risk situation that already exists. Conversely, uplift north of a line joining the Humber and Mersey estuaries will marginally reduce the risk.

## Rates of Sea-Level and Coastline Change

It is clear that relative sea level has not only risen during the Recent geological past, but has also fallen with rates of sea-level change being variable. Similarly, coastlines are unstable and have advanced and retreated on many occasions during the Holocene: in north-west England, there have been 11 periods of coastline advance and retreat during the last 9000 years (Tooley 1978, 1982). In the Fenland, there have been eight periods of coastline advance during the past 7000 years, and it has been demonstrated (Shennan 1993) that a sustained rate of relative rise of sea level of 5mm/year resulted in net coastline retreat.

In north-west England accelerated rates of sea-level rise of 34–44mm/year about 7800 years ago have been estimated (Tooley 1974, 1978, 1989) and have been correlated with the catastrophic discharge of meltwater from the Laurentide ice cap into the Atlantic Ocean via the Mississippi or the St Lawrence Seaway. The consequence of this rapid rate of sea-level rise in Germany was that between 8600 and 7100 years ago the shoreline advanced landward some 250km at a rate of 160m/year (Streif 1989). It has been suggested (Shaw 1989) that such catastrophic discharges are sufficient to raise sea level by 23cm in a few weeks and by several metres in a few years. Even after these periods of rapid sea-level rise, there were short periods of 100 to 150 years when the rate of sea-level rise exceeded 5mm/year: for example, in the coastal lowlands adjacent to Morecambe Bay there were three periods when the rate of sea-level rise was between 5 and 10mm/year: 7600–7500BP, 6300–6150BP and 5950–5800BP (Zong and Tooley, in preparation).

These periods of accelerated sea-level rise, widely recorded in the Recent geological record and from the last interglacial geological record (Streif 1990) have not been considered in the predictions of sea-level rise (Warrick and Oerlemans 1990, Wigley and Raper 1992).

# The Geoid and Sea-Level Change

The ocean surface possesses a 'topography' with swells and depressions that can be contoured using satellite altimetry. This 'topography' is defined as the geoid which is the equipotential surface of the Earth's field of gravity. Gravitational attraction is influenced by the distribution of density of materials within the crust and mantle of the Earth and by the size of ice masses.

The abstraction of water from, and restitution of water to, the world's oceans during a glacial to interglacial cycle will have a profound effect on the shape of the geoid, and particularly the position of the swells and depressions, through the massive transfers of load from ocean basins to land, the responses to loading and unloading in the upper mantle and the accumulation and melting of ice masses. Change in global sea level is neither in the same direction, nor of the same magnitude over the globe (Walcott 1972). Clark et al (1978) identified six global regions where sea-level curves for the last 6000 years were predicted showing emergence between 70°S and 52°S reaching a maximum altitude 5000 years ago and declining thereafter, whilst further north along the meridian line the altitude of the 5000-year old beach becomes progressively lower.

Clark and Primus (1987) predicted sea-level changes consequent upon the partial melting of the Greenland ice sheet and the retreat of the Antarctic ice sheet to 2100 (Figure 2.5) sufficient to raise global sea level by 100cm. The consequence of the latter is that the northern hemisphere experiences the greatest sea-level rise (Figure 2.5a) with between 110 and 115cm in Britain. The consequence of the former is that sea level would fall by up to 200cm on the north-west coast of Iceland and around Greenland because of the glacial unloading and the reduced ice mass on Greenland, whereas sea level would rise by more than 120cm in the southern Pacific and Indian Oceans, but there would be no sea-level rise in Britain from Northern Ireland and across southern Scotland. Table 2.1 shows the calculated amounts for a partial melting of the Greenland ice sheet and for a retreat of the Antarctic ice sheet.

**Table 2.1** *Predicted sea-level changes for selected sites on continental coastlines for a partial melting of the Greenland ice sheet and a retreat of the Antarctic ice sheet sufficient to raise 'eustatic' sea level by 100cm*

| Location | Sea-level rise (+) or fall (–) (cm) | |
| --- | --- | --- |
| | *Greenland* | *Antarctica* |
| London (UK) | +22.9 | +111.3 |
| Brewster (Greenland) | −1218.3 | +112.7 |
| Louisiana (USA) | +91.2 | +115.8 |
| Bangladesh | +100.5 | +108.4 |
| Filchner–Ronne (Antarctica) | +110.8 | −210.8 |
| Cape Town (South Africa) | +113.9 | +94.8 |

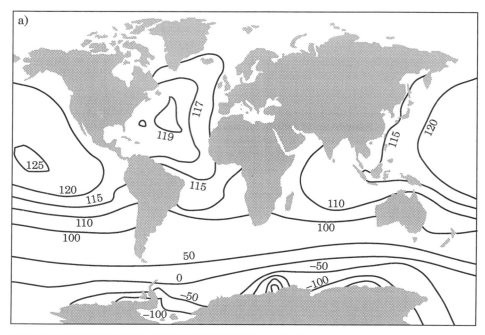

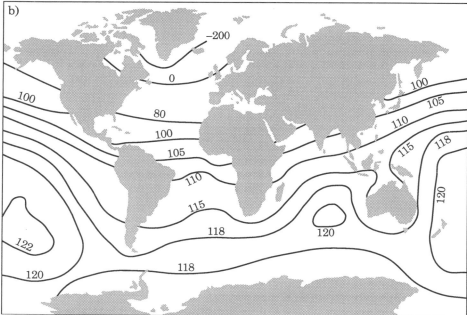

**Figure 2.5** *Maps to show the amount of sea-level rise caused by the melting of part of a) the Antarctic ice sheet, and b) the Greenland ice sheet*

Contours are in centimetres if the 'eustatic' rise of sea level is 100cm
Source: Clark and Primus 1987.

# Sea-Level Rise Scenarios

Estimates of future sea-level rise are driven by considerations of global temperature rise (steric effects, of which water expansion is the most significant) due to the addition of radiatively active gases to the Earth's atmosphere. The IPCC concluded that by 2030 global mean temperature would rise 1.1°C above 1990 temperatures and 2.5°C by 2050 (IPCC 1990a). All sea-level scenarios show that sea level rises smoothly. Hoffman (1984) gave several sea-level rise scenarios to the end of the next century ranging from 4.8cm to 56.2cm for the conservative estimate, to 17.1cm to 345cm for the high estimate. These contrast with Warrick and Oerlemans' (1990) estimate and Wigley and Raper's (1992) estimate (Figure 2.6). The scaled down estimates to 2100 are clearly shown: for the best guess for 2100 the reduction is from 66cm to 48cm, and there is the extraordinary statement in Wigley and Raper (1992, p293) that, 'changes in . . . sea level are predicted to be less severe than those estimated previously, but are still far beyond the limits of natural variability.' It is clear that this 'natural variability' refers only to the last hundred years, when spatially concentrated tide gauge data indicate a 1–2 mm/year sea-level rise (Gornitz 1993). This time period is too short, and it has been demonstrated above that rates of sea-level change have varied considerably, not only in the period prior to 7600 radiocarbon years ago, when the catastrophic discharge of meltwater led to accelerated rises in sea level in excess of 20mm/year, but also in the period up to 4000 radiocarbon years ago.

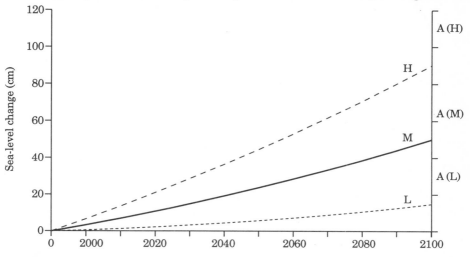

**Figure 2.6** *Global mean sea-level projections for emissions scenario 1S92a*

Thermal expansion contributions are combined with ice melt values based on low (L), middle (M) and high (H) model parameter values. The values shown on the right hand axis [A(H), A(M) and A(L)] are sea-level projections for 2100 based on the IPCC 90 'business as usual scenario' (SA90).
Source: redrawn from Wigley and Raper 1992

The failure to incorporate geoidal variations into sea-level rise predictions has resulted in a perception that sea level will rise by the same amount globally. In Britain, if a partial melting of the Greenland ice cap occurred sufficient to raise sea level by 100cm globally, sea level would fall in Scotland and rise by no more than 23cm in southern England.

If pre-7000BP sea-level rates of rise were repeated, due to catastrophic discharge of meltwater from beneath an attenuating and retreating ice cap, the rise could be achieved in a time period measured in years rather than decades and centuries. The published sea-level rise scenarios do not accommodate the range of variability of sea-level change recorded during the Recent geological past: both variable rates of change and rising and falling tendencies are characteristic.

The rates of relative sea-level rise and fall caused by earth movements, land subsidence and ground lowering due to drainage are, in some instances, greater than the predicted sea-level rise.

Extreme water levels due to astronomical and meteorological conditions, attain altitudes that are greater than any altitudes likely to be achieved if the conservative sea-level rise scenarios are realised. It is worth restating, however, that only a slight rise in regional sea level will be amplified in the frequency of extreme water levels caused by storm surges. Rossiter (1962) showed for the British coasts that a rise of mean sea level as little as 15cm would double the probability of storm surges exceeding danger level on the east coast of England and treble the probability on the west coast. Coker et al (1989) reinforced this conclusion by calculating that a 20cm rise in sea level would increase the number of storm surges equally or exceeding the danger levels specified by the Storm Tide Warning Service from 112 to 334 for the period 1972 to 1989. Storminess and the wind-wave climate consequential upon either the enhanced greenhouse effect or sunspot activity are factors of greater moment for the coasts, sea defences and coastal lowlands of Britain than posited sea-level rise.

# Economic and Policy Implications

The complexities and uncertainties surrounding the estimation of past rises and falls in sea level and the forecasting of future changes in sea level have been emphasised in the first part of this chapter. It has been shown that much of Britain's coastal lowlands are already at risk since they lie well below the present-day high-tide levels. It is also the case that coastal lowlands will become more at risk if in the future sea level rises, or if ground altitudes fall or there is an increase in storminess and hence extreme water levels.

Coastal protection and flood defence policy is the responsibility of the Ministry of Agriculture, Fisheries and Food in England and Wales. The National Rivers Authority (NRA) and local authorities are mainly responsible for the planning, execution and maintenance of works on the coast. Capital and maintenance costs are largely financed from the Treasury.

The primary aim of the sea defence policy is the reduction of loss of life or capital asset damage. The enabling measures are stated to be the provision of adequate and cost effective flood warning systems; the provision of technically, environmentally and economically sound and sustainable defence measures; and the discouragement of inappropriate development in areas at risk from flooding and coastal erosion (Ministry of Agriculture, Fisheries and Food 1993a, b).

Published 'best guess' predictions of sea-level rise are in the range of 33–39cm by the year 2050 (17–26cm by the year 2030) (see Figure 2.6, Wigley and Raper 1992). On a regional basis, the estimates are 33–39cm for the East Anglian coast and 20–23cm for north-west Scotland. The NRA, which has the responsibility for sea defences over much of the coastline of England and Wales, is currently operating on regional estimates of sea-level rise of 4–6mm per annum (Table 2.2). The most recent information (mid-1994) predicts a mean sea-level rise from 1990 of 11cm (regional variation 18.5–2cm) by 2050 and 45cm by 2100.

**Table 2.2** *NRA operational guidelines for regional sea-level rise*

| Region | Rise (mm/year) | Total rise by 2030 (over 1990 levels) (mm) |
|---|---|---|
| *Anglian, Thames and Southern* | *6* | *24* |
| *North West, Northumbria[a]* | *4* | *16* |
| *Severn Trent, South West[a]* | | |
| *Welsh, Wessex[a] and Yorkshire[a]* | *5* | *20* |

[a]Northumbria and Yorkshire, and South West and Wessex, were merged in 1993
Source: Arnell et al 1994

These future sea-level rise scenarios must, however, be treated with some caution. We have argued that these predictions have not considered a long enough past time-series record. They do not include the periods of accelerated sea-level rise and fall that are to be found in the recent geological record. The scenarios also assume that sea level rises smoothly, which may not necessarily be the case. Changes in the frequency and severity of extreme storms pose a more significant threat than sea-level rise in isolation, but climate models do not simulate small-scale disturbances such as storm systems at all accurately at the moment (Holt 1991). Some preliminary work, although far from definitive, suggested that changes in weather patterns could cause more frequent surges. It was also found that the models predicted that mobile beaches were very sensitive to even slight changes in mean wave heights and directions. The degradation or loss of beaches would have serious consequences for some coastal areas.

# Towards Integrated Coastal Management

Humans have been intervening in the coastal zone over a long period of time, and in the last two centuries this intervention in Britain has led to significant changes and exerted strong pressures on coastal processes and ecosystems via urbanisation, industrialisation and waste disposal. In 1991/92 the NRA spent over £91 million on sea-defence-related capital works to defend people, property and some natural systems (Arnell et al 1994). Most of the land lying above sea level is unlikely to be permanently flooded (by sea-level rise estimates currently being put forward) because of the defence systems that are in place. The coastline of England and Wales, for example, is approximately 4500km long and over 33 per cent, mainly in the East Anglian region, is protected by artificial (hard engineering) defences. In 1992 the NRA published the results of a survey of existing sea defences and their condition (Figure 2.7). Maintenance and replacement costs for sea defences and coastal protection works will be substantial in the future.

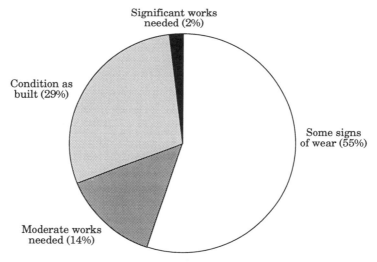

**Figure 2.7** *Condition of NRA sea defences in England*

The survey and its results are based on an examination of the separate elements of each defence, for example, walls, embankments, groynes.
Source: National Audit Office 1992, National Rivers Authority Sea Defence Survey 1990–91

Any increase in the frequency with which sea and coastal defences are overtopped or breached would have major financial implications. Flood losses during the 1953 east coast floods amounted to some £30 million in 1953 prices (equivalent to over £350 million in 1991 prices) (Arnell et al 1994). A great deal of new economic development has taken place in coastal flood risk areas since 1953. The financial value of the coastal land along the south coast of England, for example, has been estimated to be up to £5745 million (Ball et al 1991).

Current defences have to be designed against storm surges which on some North Sea coasts can exceed 2.5m. According to some analysts, predicted regional sea-level rises in parts of Britain could result in sea levels which currently have return periods of 100 years (ie annual probability of

0.01) falling to between 1 in 6 and 1 in 70 years by 2030, and to between 1 in 1 year and 1 in 20 years by 2100 (POL 1993). These predictions do not take account of any local adjustments in bathymetry during the period of rise or the change in performance of structures as a result of changes in wave climate with increased local depths of water.

The ground altitudes of Britain's coastal lowlands have been and are being further lowered because of drainage activities. Thus any climate-induced rise in sea level will serve only to exacerbate the risk that these lowlands already face. Overall, Britain's coastal zone is being altered by a combination of environmental (geological and climatic) changes and socio-economic changes, plus related feedback mechanisms. The management challenge is therefore to limit the impact of further urbanisation and economic development on adjacent 'natural' areas, while at the same time protecting coastal infrastructure and the social and economic support systems from external (for example, climate-related) stress and shock.

Complete protection may not be the appropriate policy response to sea-level rise, even if it were financially practicable. In some areas the main effect of recent sea-level rise seems to have been the steepening of beach profiles and the consequent loss of areas of inter-tidal habitat including salt marsh. Some 2750ha of salt marsh and up to 10,000ha of inter-tidal flats, which represent a significant environmental resource, may be under threat from sea-level rise (Pye and French 1993). The presence of hard engineering defences are probably the cause of this loss because they prevent the natural adjustment of the coastline (for example, landward retreat of salt marshes) as sea level increases. The solution to this is perhaps a policy of selective managed retreat where existing and/or future land uses permit (Department of the Environment 1992).

It seems clear that moves towards the longer-term objective of integrated coastal zone management are required. Such a management approach should be strategic and based on processes rather than end states. In the past in Britain there has been a lack of coordination between coastal planning and coastal defence and the prevailing opinion has been that coastal erosion and flooding were not planning issues (Lee 1993).

The British coastal zone can provide a range of use benefits but they are not all compatible with each other. Lee (1993) believes that coastal management problems can be focused down to a limited number of value and use conflicts in a few locations. These include:

- pressures arising from tourism and recreation on parts of the relatively unspoilt coastline in south and east England and south Wales;
- urban and industrial development pressures on estuaries which also provide natural capital assets of significant conservation value (for example, Cardiff Bay, the Mersey estuary, the Solent and the Thames);
- marine aggregate extraction activities and consequent increased erosion on the coastlines of south and east England and Wales;
- residential area protection and conflicting landscape conservation.

During the 1990s there have been a number of changes in the institutional framework underpinning British coastal management. The official view is that more integrated management systems will evolve from a combination of existing statutory and voluntary planning procedures (Department of the Environment 1992). Coastal groups which comprise all those bodies concerned with coastal management have been encouraged to produce shoreline management plans. These groups have been set up since 1985 as non-statutory bodies and now cover nearly all the coastline of England and Wales. There is informal coordination of these groups through a national coastal defence forum. The coastal groups have a clear role in ensuring that local authority development plans take account of coastal defence strategies. Central guidelines for the integration of coastal management issues into structure planning were issued in a 1993 Planning Policy Guidance Note (Department of the Environment 1992). All capital schemes for the reconstruction or improvement of defences have to satisfy technical, economic and environmental criteria. We now turn to an examination of the economic implications of sea-level rise and related policy responses.

## Economic Analysis

It is possible to approach the problem of assessing the economic implications of sea-level rise and the policy responses either from a 'top down' or a 'bottom up' perspective. Both approaches have been applied at a global level (for the former see IPCC 1990, 1992; and for the latter see Milliman et al 1989 and den Elzen and Rotmans 1992). The 'top down' assessment necessarily has to rely on aggregated data, but Fankhauser (1994) has recently produced such an analysis. In his model, the rule of thumb used to estimate the socially optimal degree of coastal protection is the ratio of costs under full protection against those under full retreat. The larger the costs of protection, or the lower the damage under full retreat, the lower will be the degree of protection.

Fankhauser's (1994) model predicts that for Britain the optimal degree of protection varies between 92 per cent and 98 per cent (sea-level rise 20cm up to 1m over the next 100 years) for open coasts and beaches, and between 98 per cent and 99 per cent for urban/industrial/port areas. The policy message of these tentative results is that it will probably be economically optimal for Britain to protect most of its vulnerable coastline. Provided that the cost-efficient solution is implemented, the costs of sea-level rise for Britain will not be catastrophically high. The combined protection and damage cost estimate varies between £48 billion and £283 billion (for sea-level rise of 20cm to 1m over the next 100 years); or £1.9 billion to £10.3 billion depending on which discount rate, 2 per cent or 4.4 per cent, is utilised (Fankhauser 1994).

The aggregated nature of the data and the 'top down' type model may, however, mask important regional/local differences. The optimal policy response to sea-level rise is really a problem of regional coastal zone management. Thus the optimal protection strategy will be different for different coastlines. An economic cost-benefit analysis study of Britain's most vulnerable regional coastline, the East Anglian coast, has been completed (Turner et al 1994). The study area was a stretch of coast bordering the North Sea from Hunstanton to Felixstowe (Figure 2.8). The vulnerable zone contains a range of urban/industrial and ecological (recreation, landscape and amenity) assets.

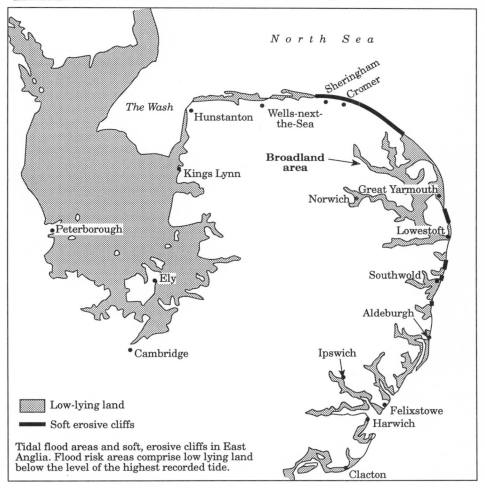

**Figure 2.8** *Low-lying land and soft cliffs in East Anglia*

The basic approach adopted in the study was to combine information about the physical hazard posed by accelerated sea-level rise with data on assets at risk in order to produce a physical/numerical, and then economic estimation of the impacts. The analysis was ordered in a stepwise manner in accord with the approach recommended by the IPCC (IPCC, CZMS 1992) (Figure 2.9).

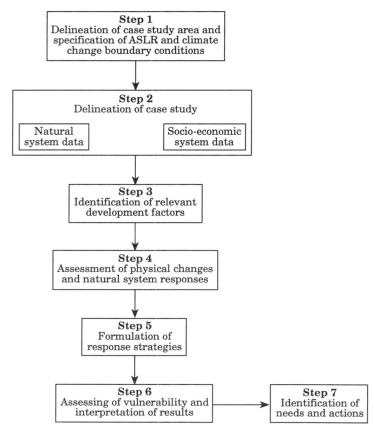

**Figure 2.9** *Stepwise approach of vulnerability analyses*

The vulnerability of this stretch of coastline derives partly from the existence of large areas of low-lying land, both immediately adjacent to the shoreline and inland of Great Yarmouth, and stretches of soft erodable cliffs. The zone also contains the complex wetland known as The Broads. The wetland is under continued threat from mainly saline flooding (which would change the existing freshwater ecosystem) with some 20,000ha lying below surge-tidal level. Coastal defences (mainly hard engineering structures) built largely after the very destructive 1953 North Sea storm surge flood, and river flood embankments require constant maintenance and renovation. The Broads, for example, are protected by over 200km of tidal embankments, many of which are old and in a deteriorating condition. The current standard of flood protection provided by the river walls in The Broads is frequently below a 1 in 10 (or even 1 in 5) -year flood return.

The results of this 'bottom up' regional analysis are broadly consistent with those of the 'top down' model described earlier. Table 2.3 summarises the costs of protecting the East Anglian hazard zone, and the net benefits value results (ie discounted protection costs minus discounted benefits of protection in terms of damage costs avoided) for the 'accommodate' and 'protect' policy options. The former option would involve the continued maintenance of the current defence system, that is a declining standard of protection over time as and when sea-level rise takes place. The latter option requires the continual upgrading of defence to keep pace with future sea-level rise.

**Table 2.3** *Costs and benefits of sea-level rise and policy responses in East Anglia (1990–2050)*

|  | Sea-level rise | (6% discount rate, £ million) | | |
|  | 20cm | 40cm | 60cm | 80cm |
| --- | --- | --- | --- | --- |
| *Protection costs:* | | | | |
| Retreat | – | – | – | – |
| Accommodate | 132 | 137 | 151 | 157 |
| Protect | 187 | 232 | 292 | 485 |
| *Damage costs avoided* | | | | |
| *(ie benefits of* | | | | |
| *defence relative to* | | | | |
| *do nothing 'retreat'):* | | | | |
| Accommodate | 1139–1141 | 1098–1108 | 1085–1098 | 1039–1058 |
| Protect | 1256–1259 | 1281–1284 | 1324–1326 | 1351–1352 |
| *Net benefits:* | | | | |
| Accommodate | 1007–1009 | 961–971 | 934–947 | 882–901 |
| Protect | 1069–1072 | 1049–1052 | 1032–1034 | 866–867 |

Source: Turner, Doktor and Adger 1994

Table 2.3 indicates that the protection strategy is the most economically efficient response on a region-wide basis. However, the study area can be divided into 184 individual flood and erosion compartments (Figure 2.10). At this disaggregated and localised scale, protection is not always the most economic response. Analysis of the 113 flood-hazard compartments indicates that as the sea-level rise predictions increase, the number of coastal sections in which retreat (ie do nothing) is the most efficient response also increases (Turner et al 1994).

In some cases the net present values of the accommodate and protect strategies were identical and in some cases the net present values of both of these 'active' responses were zero, indicating that none of the response strategies were dominant. The overall result seems to be that the optimal approach will be a combination of different localised response strategies.

It must be stressed, however, that the East Anglian study has a number of limitations. In the absence of full scientific data about the local erosion and sedimentation processes, the analysis assumed that each coastal compartment was independent of any other compartment. This is clearly a gross simplification of reality. It is also the case that human systems (as well as other natural systems) will adapt to sea-level rise. The model was only avail-

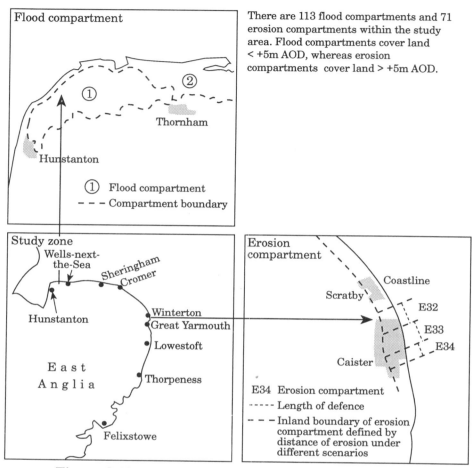

There are 113 flood compartments and 71 erosion compartments within the study area. Flood compartments cover land < +5m AOD, whereas erosion compartments cover land > +5m AOD.

**Figure 2.10** *Examples of flood and erosion compartments*

able to incorporate a limited degree of adaptive behaviour. Finally, many of the assets found to be at risk from sea-level rise could not be easily valued in economic monetary terms. Thus only the recreation and amenity value of The Broads was included in the potential environmental damage estimates.

Nevertheless, the East Anglian study does show that the CZMS 'Common Methodology' can be utilised in order to get an approximate, but meaningful, vulnerability assessment of coastal zones. The data requirements for even this simplified modelling approach have, however, been formidable.

# Conclusions

This chapter has highlighted the fact that the issue of sea-level rise and its impacts on Britain is complex and beset with a range of scientific and socio-economic uncertainties. It does, however, seem clear that British coastal lowlands are at risk and other stretches of coastline would also be at risk were it not for the defensive structures that have previously been built. Both the eastern and southern coastlines of England are already heavily defended, with their hinterlands supporting a range of valuable economic and ecological assets.

The limited economic analysis that has been carried out suggests that, with the exception of limited local stretches of coastlines, the protect response strategy is the correct economic approach. Current defensive systems, suitably maintained and improved, should be able to cope with the consequences of published best-guess estimates of future sea-level rise. But these estimates have a number of shortcomings, which were reviewed in the first half of this chapter, and the risk of combined sea-level rise and storm surge may be greater than is apparent now. Paradoxically, the continued human interventions in the coastal zone both enhance its capability to defend against external shocks, as well as contributing to increasing potential susceptibility and vulnerability trends.

# 3

# Implications for Water Supply and Water Management

## Introduction

Climate change due to global warming is likely to have significant impacts on hydrological regimes, with consequent implications for water resources and the management of water. There have been many studies of potential changes in hydrological regimes in many environments, and a few studies of impacts on water management systems. However, there has been very little work on the economic implications of possible changes. This chapter aims to summarise how the water industry in Britain might be affected by changes in hydrological regimes, and explores the potential economic consequences of both the impacts and management responses. In order to do this, the chapter needs to develop a methodological framework for considering the economic impacts of change.

## The Context

### Water Management in Britain

Since 1989 water management in England and Wales has been undertaken by a mixture of private and public organisations. Privately owned companies provide public water supplies and treat waste water, under the regulation of the National Rivers Authority (NRA) and the Office of Water Services (OFWAT). All abstractions from, and discharges to, water courses and groundwater must be licensed by the NRA, which has statutory responsibilities not only to preserve the integrity of water resources for human use, but also to maintain and improve the quality of the water environment. The

NRA is the agency through which the Department of the Environment ensures compliance with British and European Union legislation (on, for example, water quality standards). The NRA also has powers to provide defence against coastal and river flooding, and to prevent pollution of water courses and aquifers. OFWAT regulates the financial aspects of water management, through powers to limit water company price increases and set limits on returns from capital investment.

A rather different structure exists in Scotland, lying wholly within the public sector. Here, the responsibility for water supply, sewerage and sewage treatment lies with nine regional councils and three islands councils, together with the Central Scotland Water Development Board. Pollution control and flood defence are carried out by seven catchment-based river purification boards.

## Current Water Management Issues in Britain

There are currently three major water management issues in Britain, and each is likely to be affected by climate change.

The first concerns the balancing of water supply with water demand. Figure 3.1 shows current abstractions as a percentage of the total water available in a drought (the amount which can actually be supplied with current water supply systems is less than the total water available). It is clear from the figure that available resources are under considerable pressure in the south and east of England: in the Thames region current abstractions are greater than the drought water availability (although water is recycled). The figure hides considerable variability in resource pressure both within a region and during the year. The influx of tourists to the South West in summer, for example, results in high summer demands. It is in the regions with greatest pressures that demand is expected to increase the fastest. The NRA forecast an increase of up to 37 per cent in the Anglian Region (NRA 1994).

Options for alleviating these pressures include providing new supplies (through measures such as the increased exploitation of groundwater, the construction of new reservoirs or the transfer of water from water-rich areas) and restricting the increase in demand (through water metering, for example). Each option has economic, environmental and political costs (NRA 1994).

The second major issue facing the water industry relates to water quality. The industry is currently spending large sums to improve the treatment of sewage effluent, and the NRA is introducing measures to limit the build up of nitrates and pesticides in drinking water. These efforts are a direct response to European Union directives on drinking water quality.

The third issue is the prevention of flood damages. Flooding during the winter of 1993/94 has illustrated once more the vulnerability of British towns and cities to flooding, and has emphasised the value of the large capital investment that has been made by the NRA and its predecessors over many decades. A major investment programme is currently under way to

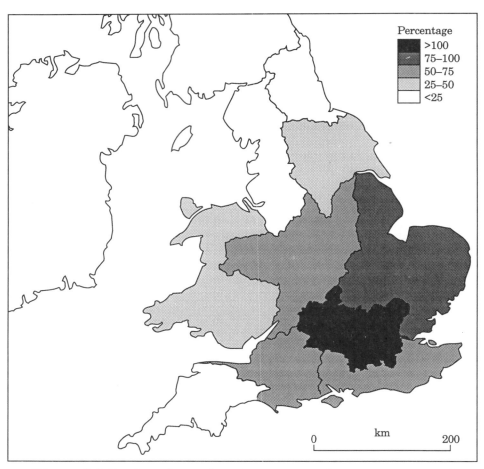

**Figure 3.1** *Current abstractions for water supply as a percentage of drought rainfall*

Sources: Abstractions from Water Services Assocation 1993, 50-year effective rainfall from NRA 1991a

renovate the coastal defences along the east coast of England, which are now reaching the end of their design lives.

Underpinning all three issues is the increasing emphasis placed by the NRA (and legislators) on the environmental aspects of water management, and particularly on environmental protection. This emphasis manifests itself in several ways. Specific water management schemes are designed to minimise their impact on the environment, and environmental considerations affect management decisions. Some actions are taken specifically to enhance environmental quality.

# Climate Change, Hydrological Regimes and Water Resources

## Introduction

It is not possible to predict with any reliability the detailed pattern of climate over the next few decades, so any assessment of the possible effects of climate change must use feasible scenarios. Scenarios for possible future climates can be derived from interpretation of historical records, but most climate change impact assessments now use scenarios based on the results of climate simulation models (General Circulation Models: GCMs). The discussion in this chapter is based on the CCIRG scenarios of climate change (see Chapter 1, Arnell and Reynard 1993, CCIRG 1991). The best CCIRG scenario assumes an increase in winter rainfall and no change in summer rainfall, the wettest assumes an increase throughout the year, and the driest assumes no change in winter but a reduction in summer. The effect of the change in rainfall is compounded by increased potential evaporation. Depending on assumptions about changes in meteorological characteristics, annual potential evaporation is assumed to increase by between 5 per cent and 28 per cent (Arnell and Reynard 1993).

The basic methodology underpinning most hydrological and water resources impact studies is as follows: input series of climate data under current and future conditions are fed into a hydrological simulation model, and the simulated flows and groundwater levels are passed into a model of the water management system. The impacts of changes in inputs can be expressed in terms ranging from changes in monthly runoff to changes in the frequency of demand restrictions or exceedance of European Union water quality limits. It is also possible to compare the effects of climate change with those of other changes, such as economic development or land use change. Another approach is to work backwards, and determine the degree of change which would be needed to cause some impact of a magnitude that exceeds some agreed measure of significance.

General reviews of the implications of climate change for water resources and water management in Britain are given in Arnell et al (1994) and Arnell (1994). Before describing possible changes in hydrological and water resources characteristics in Britain, it is important to make a few general points.

First, the estimated changes are very dependent on the assumed changes in precipitation and evaporation: predictions are very uncertain. Second, the impact of a given climate change varies considerably between catchments and water management systems. Geological conditions and current climatic characteristics affect changes in runoff, and the implications for a water resources system are dependent on the pressures currently faced by that system. A system with a large degree of slack will be better able to cope with climate change than one which is already highly stressed. Third, the variability in impact between catchments and systems means it is difficult to extrapolate results from one study to another. Fourth, there are a number of steps in the relationship between climate change and impact. A system may be able to cope with change up to a certain point, but might fail with a greater change; the link between climate and impact is non-linear.

## Change in Water Resources

Figure 3.2 shows the percentage change in average annual runoff in Britain by 2050, under the CCIRG-based climate change scenarios (Arnell and Reynard 1993). The changes were produced by simulating runoff in each grid square using a simple hydrological water balance model. The maps show not only the spatial variability in impact (the percentage change in runoff is generally greater in the drier south and east of Britain), but also the large differences between scenarios. Scenario PE1 has the lowest increase in potential evaporation (around 5 per cent) whilst PE2 has the highest (up to 28 per cent). Under the driest, most extreme scenario, runoff across most of England would be reduced by up to 30 per cent, with the greatest decrease in the south and east. Runoff under most scenarios would increase in the north and west.

Changes in monthly flow, however, are larger than changes in annual totals (Arnell and Reynard 1993). In general, flows increase in winter and decrease in summer under all but the wettest CCIRG scenarios, resulting in a greater variability in flow through the year and a greater change in resource availability than implied by the change in annual runoff. Figure 3.3 shows change in monthly runoff for four catchments, under the four change scenarios shown in Figure 3.2 (the central light bar defines the changes under the best CCIRG rainfall scenario, with two PE scenarios; the high and low extremes represent the wettest and driest CCIRG scenarios respectively). The large reduction in runoff in April in catchment 25006 reflects the almost complete elimination of snowfall and hence snowmelt. Winter precipitation runs off earlier in a warmer world. Summer runoff in each catchment is reduced under all the scenarios.

Groundwater is a very important source of water in south and east England. Recharge starts during autumn once soil moisture deficits have been filled, and ends in spring when evaporation begins to exceed rainfall. Higher winter rainfall would imply increased recharge, but increased evaporation would suggest a shorter recharge season. The actual effect of climate change on groundwater recharge would therefore depend on the precise balance between increased rainfall and a shorter season. Hewett et al (1993) simulated an increase in recharge in a Kent chalk aquifer, but different scenarios could have resulted in a decrease.

The frequency of drought conditions in Britain is determined by the rate of occurrence of sustained dry spells, and particularly by the occurrence of drier than average winters. Most climate models suggest an increase in

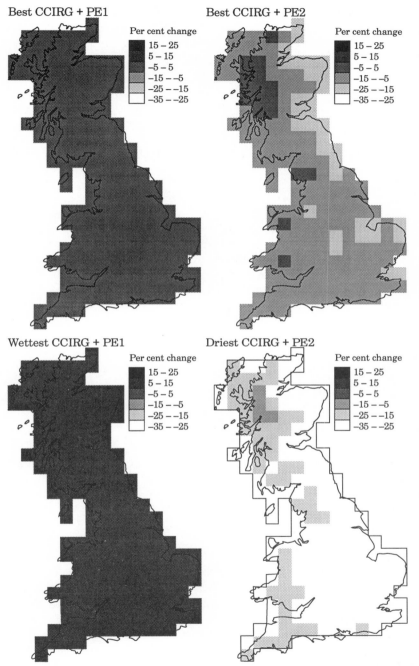

***Figure 3.2*** *Percentage change in average annual runoff by 2050 under four climate change scenarios*

Source: Arnell and Reynard 1993

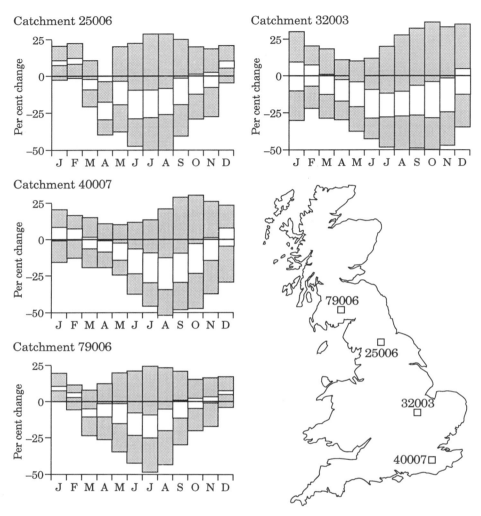

**Figure 3.3** *Percentage change in monthly runoff under four climate change scenarios for four catchments*

Source: Arnell and Reynard 1993

average winter rainfall in Britain, but it is conceivable that the frequency of low-rainfall winters could increase. Stronger anticyclonic conditions over continental Europe could force rain-bearing systems further to the north and away from southern Britain, as happened during the dry winter of 1988/89 (Arnell et al 1993). Unfortunately, it is currently not possible to determine reliably changes in storm tracks and the occurrence of dry winters from climate models, at the high spatial resolution required. Even with an increase in winter rainfall, however, higher temperatures and lower summer rainfall will increase exposure to summer drought. Extreme low flows may be reduced by over 50 per cent (Arnell and Reynard 1993).

Demand for water in Britain is generally increasing, due largely to an increase in per capita domestic consumption and demands for spray irrigation. These increases are offset to a certain extent by reduced industrial demands in heavy industry and in some regions. Herrington and Hoschatt (1993) predicted a 21 per cent increase in per capita domestic demand between 1990 and 2021 in the absence of climate change, and estimated that higher temperatures would add another 5 per cent, essentially due to increased garden use (assuming no change in pricing and metering policies). They also estimated that global warming would add 6 per cent to the increase in total demand in south and east England, equivalent to nearly 5 per cent of the amount currently put into public supply in the region.

Taken together, these changes imply increased pressures on water resources in Britain in the future, with considerable variability in impact across the country depending on geographic location and the characteristics of the water supply system. Direct river abstractions (accounting for approximately a third of all abstractions in England and Wales) would be particularly affected by large changes in seasonal – especially summer – runoff, whilst impacts on reservoir systems would depend on the amount of storage available to hold any additional winter surplus.

## Change in Water Quality

The quality of river water is a function of the amount of inputs washed in from the land surface and deposited from the atmosphere, the volume of water in the river, and the rate of operation of biological and chemical processes in the river (Jenkins et al 1993). All of these might change in the future, and interactions between these factors make it difficult to make generalised assessments.

Trends in water quality in England and Wales between 1958 and 1990 are shown in Table 3.1. The data are not strictly comparable because of changes in survey methodology over the period. However, a very gradual improvement can be discerned, with a decline in the number of very polluted rivers, although some deterioration was experienced between 1985 and 1990, concentrated mainly in the south and east. Amongst a range of causes cited for this were the two hot, dry summers in the late 1980s, and increased pressure from sewage works discharges (NRA 1991b).

Simulation studies in a few case study catchments have indicated that changes in river water temperature and river flow regimes due to climate change would generally have relatively little impact on water quality in Britain, and that changes in inputs of pollutants to the river system – determined to a considerable extent by agricultural practices – would be more important (Jenkins et al 1993). With no change in nitrogen inputs, nitrate concentrations would be more affected by changes in flow volumes than water temperature, and would probably decrease (although there is potential for increased nitrate peaks following flushing after prolonged dry spells and

*Table 3.1* Water quality in England and Wales 1958–90

| Class | Former classifications 1958–80 surveys Non-tidal rivers and canals | | | | | | | |
|---|---|---|---|---|---|---|---|---|
| | *1958* | | *1970* | | *1975* | | *1980* | |
| | *km* | *%* | *km* | *%* | *km* | *%* | *km* | *%* |
| Unpolluted | 24,950 | 72 | 28,500 | 74 | 28,810 | 75 | 28,810 | 75 |
| Doubtful | 5,220 | 15 | 6,270 | 17 | 6,730 | 17 | 7,110 | 18 |
| Poor | 2,270 | 7 | 1,940 | 5 | 1,770 | 5 | 2,000 | 5 |
| Grossly polluted | 2,250 | 6 | 1,700 | 4 | 1,270 | 3 | 810 | 2 |
| *Total* | *34,690* | | *38,400* | | *38,590* | | *38,740* | |

| | New classification 1980–90 surveys Freshwater rivers and canals | | | | | |
|---|---|---|---|---|---|---|
| | *1980*[a] | | *1985* | | *1990* | |
| | *km* | *%* | *km* | *%* | *km* | *%* |
| Good 1a | 13,830 | 34 | 13,470 | 33 | 12,408 | 26 |
| Good 1b | 14,220 | 35 | 13,990 | 34 | 14,536 | 34 |
| Fair 2 | 8,670 | 21 | 9,730 | 24 | 10,750 | 25 |
| Poor 3 | 3,260 | 8 | 3,560 | 9 | 4,022 | 9 |
| Bad 4 | 640 | 2 | 650 | 2 | 662 | 2 |
| *Total* | *40,630* | | *41,390* | | *42,434* | |

a as revised in 1985
Source: NRA 1991b

higher mineralisation of organic nitrogen in the soil). Biochemical oxygen demand is likely to decrease in clean rivers, due to higher water temperature, but would increase in rivers currently heavily utilised for effluent disposal because of increased growth of algal blooms. An increase in biochemical oxygen demand would have adverse consequences for fish and other aquatic populations. Increases in abstractions (as mentioned in the previous section) mean higher effluent discharges, exaggerating the direct climate change effects on lowland river biochemical oxygen demand and aquatic ecosystems.

## Change in River Flood Risk

Floods in Britain arise from prolonged periods of heavy rain, from short bursts of very intense rain, or from the melting of a large snow pack. Generally wetter conditions in winter under climate change would appear to increase the risk of flooding, although no numerical simulations have yet been completed. GCM predictions of changes in the rate of occurrence of intense short-duration rainfalls are very uncertain, but meteorological experience suggests that an increase in stable anticyclonic conditions in summer would lead to a greater frequency of summer thunderstorms. Higher temperatures would mean less snow and hence imply a lower risk of snow-melt flooding, but this might be offset by changes in winter precipitation totals and the origin of winter storms. Clearly, it is currently very difficult to estimate possible changes in flood risk, although initial indications are that risk will be increased. A small change in flood characteristics can have a very large effect on the risk of a specific threshold being crossed. With an increase in the mean flood magnitude of just 10 per cent, the flood currently exceeded once in 100 years on average could occur as frequently as once in 50 years (Arnell et al 1994).

# Economic Implications of Climate Change

## The Alternative Responses

The above discussion suggests that, however uncertain they might be, the economic implications of climate change for water management will in general be adverse. These economic impacts will depend on how the water industry responds to climate change. There are three basic management responses: business as usual, be defensive, or adapt.

The 'business as usual' response means that there would be no change in management practice in direct response to climate change, and that operational and investment expenditures and policies would be unaffected. The strategy implies acceptance of the reductions in standards which could accompany climate change, so that the costs of climate change are given by the value of these reductions in service standard or the loss of uses which would no longer be possible. A lower level of service might imply that the water environment, broadly defined, is no longer suitable for some economic uses, or that some uses are now provided at a lower quality (and, therefore, value). No changes in planned expenditure are deemed worthwhile under this approach, even though, for instance, the value of some of these uses might exceed the extra resource expenditure required to regain them.

This scenario can be presented diagrammatically in Figure 3.4. Under the current economically efficient situation, the pre-climate change standard of service $Qp$ is provided. Here, the marginal cost of provision ($MC.pre$) is just equal to the marginal value ($MV$), at $p$. Climate change (by, say, 2050) has the effect of lowering the standard of service which can be provided for a given expenditure. In Figure 3.4, this is shown by an upwards shift in the supply cost curve, from MC.pre to MC.post (in other words, it becomes more expensive to supply water under conditions of greater scarcity). With no change in management practice, marginal expenditures on service provision are unaffected, resulting in a lower standard of service, $Qn$. But at this point, the marginal value of provision, $n$, is greater than the cost. The costs of a 'business as usual' scenario are given by the shaded area A, which represents all those valuable economic uses which are incorrectly deemed too costly under the 'business as usual' strategy (this simplified analysis assumes that the marginal value of water remains constant after climate change: in practice, the $MV$ curve could shift too).

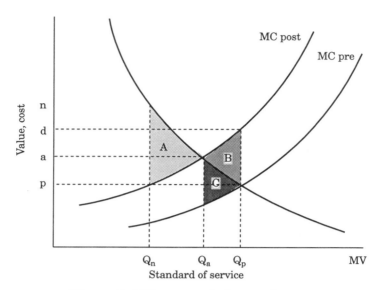

**Figure 3.4** *The costs of climate change*

A 'defensive' response is at the other end of the spectrum: it is represented by a strategy which aims to ensure that no decline in service levels would occur as a result of climate change. This strategy envisages an increase in the levels of operational and investment expenditures which would have existed without climate change in order to provide the same reliability of service or volume of water. In terms of Figure 3.4, marginal expenditure rises from p to d, maintaining service levels at Qp. It is assumed that these extra expenditures are provided efficiently; that is, that service levels are maintained at the least cost of economic resources. Then, the costs of climate change are given by the costs of 'replacing' economic uses, and returning remaining uses to their former quality. This is despite the fact that the value of such restoration might not, in some cases, justify the extra expenditure. These costs are shown by the shaded area B in Figure 3.4, which is the excess expenditure which is not justified by the value (MV) of the services provided (again assuming no change in MV).

Both the 'business as usual' and the 'defensive' responses take only a partial view of economic implications of climate change. The 'business as usual' approach ignores the fact that some uses which are lost as a result of climate change might in fact be sufficiently valuable to justify the extra expenditure required to restore them. Implicitly, then, all marginal uses of the water environment have no value under this approach. This unrealistic assumption can be expected to lead to under-investment in the water sector generally.

On the other hand, by ensuring that all uses of the water environment are maintained as climate change occurs, no matter what the cost, the defensive strategy implies that all marginal uses are at least as valuable as the cost of their restoration. This is unlikely to be the case in practice, especially given the presence in the water sector of continually rising costs of service expansion and improvement. Over-investment will be the problem in this case.

An 'adaptive' strategy attempts to steer a middle path between these two extremes, and combine elements of both. It would involve an explicit comparison of the benefits of service restoration or maintenance in the face of global warming with the extra costs that this would imply. Hence, unlike the other two approaches, adaptation makes no prior (extreme) assumptions about the size of these costs and benefits. Ultimately, the aim would be to provide a level of service after climate change where the costs of provision were just balanced at the margin by the resulting benefits. It is then, of course, tantamount to an economic cost-benefit approach to climate change response. Because of the positive (and likely rising) costs of service provision, adaptation would not generally recommend the maintenance of all the uses of the water environment which might be threatened by climate change. However, by recognising the positive value that these uses can have, it would lead to a higher level of service provision than that implied if climate change elicited no management response. Hence, service provision under adaptation ($Qa$ in Figure 3.4), is lower than would prevail under a defensive strategy $Qp$, but is higher than if no management response was forthcoming, $Qn$. Moreover, at $Qa$, the marginal cost and marginal value of service provision are equalised at a, the economically optimum outcome.

Are there any economic costs of climate change under an adaptive strategy? The initial position, $Qp$, could be compared with the adaptive position after climate change, $Qa$. Then the shaded area C is the loss in economic surplus which arises because resources become more scarce, and therefore more costly, as climate change occurs. These are the 'damage' costs which can be ascribed to activities which lead to global warming. Note that they are different in nature to the costs identified above under the other two strategies. These other costs were a reflection of the inefficiency of each strategy considered. Adaptation is an efficient strategy, but still entails costs. But they are costs brought about by activities outside the water sector, not by the management strategy itself.*

Of course, the difference between theory and practice is, more often than not, significant, and this is also the case in the water sector. The NRA employs a management system based largely on physical standards and measurements applied to water abstraction and quality. This automatically imparts a certain rigidity to management objectives because of the difficulty in trading off conflicting outcomes which are measured in different units. This is reinforced by the fact that the Water Act 1989 included in the NRA's remit a specific objective of achieving 'sustainable water use', which can be interpreted as requiring physical and/or economic indicators of environmental quality in the water sector to be at least constant over time (see Dubourg 1993, 1994a). The result is a tendency to adopt a management approach which is closer to being 'defensive' than to either the 'business as usual' or

---

* In fact, such damage costs occur also in both the 'business as usual' and 'defensive' cases, but have been omitted here for ease of exposition.

'adaptive' options just outlined. In what follows, therefore, the implications of climate change for the water sector will be considered on the assumption that such a strategy, or something approaching it, will be pursued in practice.

The lack of an economic basis to the practice of water management also creates the possibility that objectives might be achieved inefficiently, or even that they might not be achieved at all (Dubourg and Pearce 1994). Although an argument can be made for emphasising physical indicators when setting sustainability objectives in the water sector, the achievement of those objectives remains an economic problem, so that economics and sustainability need to be viewed as complementary policy criteria for management purposes (Dubourg 1994b).

## Impacts on Water Resources

Figure 3.1 showed how water resources in England and Wales are already under considerable pressure from abstractors, most particularly in the south and east of England. This is based on a comparison of gross abstraction (ie ignoring water returned) with total resources available during a 1-in-50-year drought. This regional imbalance is expected to be exacerbated, as the currently stressed areas are likely to experience the greatest reduction in annual and seasonal runoff (in percentage terms), and the greatest increase in demand. The predicted increase in demand for water – irrespective of climate change – means that many regions are already making plans for significant capital investment programmes to increase water storage and supply capacity.

A strict defensive water resources strategy would seek to continue to supply the water demanded, with a given level of reliability. It would also seek to meet those demand increases accompanying climate change (for example greater demand for spray irrigation), as well as any increases occurring through the normal processes of economic growth. It would do this by altering system operating procedures or, if this was not sufficient, increasing the amount of effective supply by increasing capacity and reducing leakages. A more flexible defensive strategy – bordering on an adaptive strategy – would attempt to curb average or peak demand through such demand management measures as incentive pricing. Current NRA policy for managing water supply over the next few decades contains this mix of capacity increase, leakage reduction and demand management (NRA 1994). A true adaptive strategy would construct a water supply system in which the costs of providing the service were just equal at the margin to the benefits gained by the users of water (and hence equal to the price they would be willing to pay).

The financial expenditures implied by a defensive strategy could be substantial. Table 3.2 presents some engineering estimates of the costs of capacity expansion projects for the Thames and Anglian regions of England and Wales. These projects range from the expanded exploitation of groundwater, to the artificial reuse of effluent and the large-scale transfer of water from other regions. As Table 3.2 shows, many millions, sometimes billions, of pounds are involved. Maintaining existing supplies and meeting increases in demand could obviously be a costly endeavour.

*Table 3.2* *Supply expansion in Thames and Anglian regions*

| Example options | Yield Ml/d | Present value of cost of expansion (£m) | Marginal capital cost (£/Ml/d) |
|---|---|---|---|
| *Local schemes* | | | |
| Groundwater pumping | 235 | 75 | 28,000 |
| Effluent reuse | 150 | 126 | 36,000 |
| Reservoir | 200 | 310 | 138,000 |
| *Tranfer schemes* | | | |
| North–South | 800 | 1,200 | 131,000 |
| East–West | 1,000 | 1,400 | 114,000 |
| Reservoir | | | 131,000 |
| Current implicit | | Thames | £1,700 |
| abstraction price (£/Ml/d) | | Anglian | £3,200 |

Source: based on Dubourg 1994a

What would be the economic value of a defensive strategy? Water abstraction has a value derived from uses to which the water can be put, whether industrial, agricultural or domestic. It is assumed that water users are able to abstract as much as they wish at current prices, given the obligation of the water industry to meet all 'reasonable' demands, and the interpretation of 'reasonable' that has generally been employed in practice. Then the marginal value of water is approximated by the current price paid for it (Trigg and Dubourg 1993). Estimates of the current implicit prices for one megalitre of water abstraction per day (Ml/d), based on existing NRA charging formulae (for example, NRA 1993) are also given in Table 3.2. Comparing these with the appropriate estimates of the marginal cost of expansion (marginal capital cost) reveals that the economic supply price of water is currently approximately ten times greater than its marginal valuation in the Anglian region, and 20 times greater in Thames. Clearly, then, a defensive strategy based on these types of investment projects could be extremely costly in economic terms.

Of course, a variety of other approaches is available for increasing the effective availability of water. Water savings through leakage control are often cited as one of the most cost-effective ways of meeting increased demands (for example, NRA 1992). Currently, 'unaccounted for water' ranges from around 16 per cent of total water abstracted to over 30 per cent in some regions, with investment costs in the region of £20,000/Ml/d (NRA 1991c). Using the methodology employed by Dubourg (1994c), these figures translate into estimates of marginal capital cost of around £1,800/Ml/d. Although the operating costs of current and expanded supply still need to be included to arrive at a full supply price for water (still excluding any environmental costs, however), it is clear that leakage control is considerably cheaper than capacity increase (although the cost of leakage control will increase as the cheapest leaks are plugged first).

The effects of tariff structures and incentive charging on the demand for water are currently uncertain and the subject of considerable research within the water industry. However, raising prices immediately to long-run marginal cost levels might reduce current abstraction demand by 10–15 per cent, even under seemingly very undemanding assumptions about the responsiveness of demand to price changes (Dubourg 1994c). This would relieve considerably the stresses on resource availability in both the Thames and Anglian regions, as well as providing savings through the postponement of costly investment projects.

In sum, a defensive strategy towards water supply management in the face of climate change is likely to involve considerable costs, both financial and economic. This is because management and investment planning has emphasised predominantly engineering solutions to the problem of balancing supply and demand. As capital projects become increasingly expensive, the costs of such an approach will rise. A more economic approach to water supply, whether through incentive charging or other mechanisms such as netback analysis* (for example, see Bate and Dubourg 1994), could therefore yield large savings, both now and in the future.

## Impacts on Water Quality

Water quality management in England and Wales currently comprises two principal tools. Informal river quality objectives (RQOs), soon to be replaced by statutory water quality objectives (SWQOs), define a range of use-related water quality classes in terms of a number of biochemical determinants, including biological oxygen demand and dissolved oxygen. Discharges to controlled waters are governed by a system of consents which specify the maximum permitted volume, content and destination of the discharge. Consents are issued to dischargers so long as this would not result in RQOs not being met. A charge is levied on each consent, related to the discharge characteristics specified therein. Enforcement of the conditions surrounding consents is via prosecution in the courts, although most enforcement in practice is of the informal, 'persuasive' kind.

Even without climate change, for those waters with little quality-buffering because water quality limits are already binding on further consent demands, a policy to maintain water quality within existing RQOs

---

* Netback analysis is an allocation tool frequently used by organisations such as the World Bank. It compares estimates of the value of water in particular uses (eg from industry data) with estimates of the true marginal cost of water supply. A potential use passes the netback test if the value is at least as great as the supply cost. The granting of an abstraction licence can then be justified.

would require either or both of the following: a reduction in effluent currently discharged (probably through the revocation of certain consents), and an improvement in the quality of effluent discharged to receiving waters. The economic costs of climate change in this case are the direct costs of increased pollution abatement (through either treatment or changes in management practice), and the value of activities which must cease because they are not viable in the face of these extra direct costs. It is, unfortunately, difficult to arrive at quantitative estimates of these costs, although sums spent on treatment and abatement can be very large. For instance, OFWAT estimates that water companies in England and Wales will have to spend more than £7 billion over the period 1989 to 1995 to improve discharges from sewage treatment works and storm overflows (OFWAT 1991).

The benefits of maintaining water quality at existing RQOs, resisting the downward pressure of climate change, depend on current quality and the extent to which quality would otherwise be expected to fall. Some evidence suggests that benefits associated with generally improved amenity and recreation tend to be concentrated at lower quality levels where improvements are more easily discerned by the general public (Coughlin 1976). This would imply that there was little benefit from these sources in maintaining rivers at high quality levels. (Even if individual valuations are small, however, aggregate benefits can still be substantial if large numbers of people are affected.) On the other hand, expenditure on activities such as angling can be significant (generating revenue of more than £15 million in 1985 for the case of Welsh salmonoid fisheries, for instance (Welsh Water 1985)). Clearly, then, the benefits of maintaining water quality will also depend on, among other things, the current use of the river, its location, and the number of people affected.

The previous discussion suggested that some reduction in standards would probably be justified in the face of the adverse impacts of climate change. Such a result is still sustainable even if 'sustainable water use' requires that water quality should not decline over time (for example Dubourg 1994a,b, Herrington 1990). This is because sustainability imposes constraints only upon activity within the system which is to be sustained: climate change constitutes an exogenous change in the characteristics of the water environment, rather than a 'symptom' of unsustainable behaviour within the water sector.

However, even if a defensive strategy were economically justified (perhaps because original water quality standards were already too low), its implementation would probably not be cost-effective, because policy instruments currently in use for water quality management are inefficient. Most importantly, unlike market-based instruments such as incentive charges and tradeable permits, the 'first-come, first-served' allocation of discharge consents takes no account of the often substantial variation in pollution abatement costs across polluters. Some polluters for whom abatement is extremely costly might be obliged to cut back because discharge consents have already been allocated to other dischargers who could abate much more cheaply. In certain cases, this failure could account for up to 90 per cent of the costs of achieving water quality objectives (Hanley 1992), and is often cited as the primary advantage of market-based instruments as policy tools.

It has been suggested (for example, Kelman 1981) that environmentalists and others are as concerned with motives as with outcomes, and often oppose market-based instruments on the grounds that they appear to legitimise polluting activities. This raises the intriguing ethical dilemma of whether it is necessary to accept 'ethical' policies which are more costly and less effective than their 'unethical' economic counterparts (Kneese and Schulze 1985, Dubourg and Pearce 1994). While this probably plays down the extent to which regulation can be tailored to approximate more closely to the economic approach, it serves to underline the importance of appraising both policy objectives and regulatory instruments with a more economic eye.

## Impacts on Environmental Hazards

The NRA has target standards of service, and aims to give different land uses specific levels of protection. A change in flood characteristics would change standards enjoyed by floodplain land users.

A defensive strategy would be to improve flood protection works (flood walls, bypass channels, storage areas), and the costs would be the costs of the additional construction or maintenance. The costs of a do-nothing strategy would be equal to the additional flood losses incurred in the future. These costs can in principle readily be estimated using the standard economic assessment procedures currently used in the evaluation of flood protection schemes (Parker et al 1987). The costs of climate change would be the difference between the present value of flood losses under current conditions, and the present value of losses under changed flood regimes.

An adaptive strategy would compare the costs and benefits of different responses to climate change, and the costs would be dependent on the change in flood losses and costs of remedial actions.

# Conclusions

The economic implications of climate change for water management in Britain depend on two main factors: the impacts of climate change on hydrological conditions in the water sector, and the management strategy adopted in response to these impacts. On balance, climate change will most likely have impacts which are adverse, increasing the costs of achieving any particular standard of service. The probable management response will be largely defensive, with service levels being maintained as far as possible in the face of these changes, at the lowest economic and environmental cost. This approach is likely because of the importance of defined standards – environmental and legislative – in current water management. However, a strict adaptive response, whereby the economic costs and benefits of action are compared and the most economically efficient strategy is chosen, would minimise the economic costs of climate change.

Two major areas of uncertainty have also become apparent in the discussion. The first is that it is very difficult to predict with confidence changes in hydrological regimes which might accompany a warming of the Earth's atmosphere. To be sure, the science and modelling of climate change and associated impacts is still developing, and the likelihood of 'Type II' errors can be expected to diminish as this learning process continues. However, the inherent complexity and chaotic behaviour of natural systems mean that predictions of future hydrological regimes will be very uncertain.

But even if climate change impacts could be predicted with absolute certainty, the economic implications would still be difficult to quantify. This is not so much a result of the uncertainty surrounding the selection of a response strategy, but rather because of the continued general lack of information about the economic costs and benefits of water service provision. In the past, management practice in the water sector has been based primarily on engineering principles, so that there has been little need for economic information. As water service provision becomes more costly, however, especially with climate change, the justification for an economic approach to water management increases. Unfortunately, this information deficit limits the extent to which economics-based policies can be adopted.

Finally, it is clear that there is considerable scope for research into the potential economic implications of changes in water availability. There are many methodological issues to address (clarifying, for example, the 'business as usual', 'defensive' and adaptive approaches), and there are practical problems in estimating economic impacts. For example, how can costs, benefits and economically efficient strategies be estimated under an *evolving* climate, and what is the most appropriate baseline against which costs of climate change can be assessed? Such research will help in the formulation of appropriate – and economically efficient – response strategies.

# 4

# Implications for Agriculture and Land Use

The purpose of this chapter is to evaluate the range of potential effects of climate change on agriculture in Britain, particularly those of an economic rather than a purely biophysical nature. An initial outline is given of the magnitude and geographical pattern of changes in climate that might occur in the 21st century. This is followed by an analysis of the spatial shifts of agro-climatic potential, at both the European and British scales. There then follows an evaluation of possible changes in crop yield, particularly for wheat. Finally, the chapter is concerned with the effects that climate-induced changes in agricultural production at the global level may have on agricultural commodity prices and, through these, on land use allocations in England and Wales.

## Scenarios of Future Change in Climate

The sections that follow will consider impacts on agriculture under a variety of different scenarios of climate change. Some of these will be so-called 'synthetic' scenarios, where increments of change to temperature (T) and precipitation (P) are taken (for example, T+2°C, P+/–10 per cent). Others are based on outputs of experiments with general circulation models (GCMs).

Results from three experiments with the Goddard Institute for Space Studies (GISS) GCM (labelled scenarios A, B and C) are employed in this study and are compared with a hundred-year control simulation, which assumes 1958 levels of greenhouse gas concentrations (Hansen et al 1988). Results are also available for other GCMs (Geophysical Fluid Dynamics Laboratory (GFDL) and United Kingdom Meteorological Office (UKMO)), but for reasons of space, cannot be reported here (Carter et al 1991a, 1991b).

Scenario A, conducted for the period 1958–2062, assumes that greenhouse gas emissions continue to rise at the accelerating growth rates typical of the 1970s and 1980s. An equivalent-doubling of $CO_2$ is achieved under this scenario in about 2030. Scenario B (1958–2029) allows for decreasing rates of growth in greenhouse gas emissions such that the annual increase of radiative forcing remains approximately constant at the present level. Under this scenario, equivalent $CO_2$ doubling would be reached in about 2060. Finally, scenario C (1958–2039) assumes drastic reductions in emissions growth between 1990 and 2000 such that radiative forcing is stabilised after 2000 and equivalent-doubling of $CO_2$ is never reached (Hansen et al 1988).

It has been suggested that GISS scenario A, giving a global warming between the years 1958 and 2030 of about 2.1°C, represents a useful upper boundary to future warming over the next few decades (Rowntree 1990). In contrast, the GISS scenario C indicates a global warming of nearly 1°C over the same period (Hansen et al 1988). This rate of change is comparable to that reported (based on a range of criteria) as constituting a possible lower limit on future global warming (Rowntree 1990). To illustrate the GISS model transient projection for a single location in Europe, changes in decadal mean seasonal temperature estimated for scenarios A, B and C at a grid point in northern Sweden are depicted in Figure 4.1. Note that, as calculations were made for decadal averages, reference to decades (for example the 1990s) can be interpreted as the mid-point of the decade (ie 1995). Also plotted is the hundred-year control simulation, to show how the warming signal compares with model estimates of present-day variability.

# Changes in the Location of Crop Suitability in Europe

One of the more obvious effects of possible greenhouse gas-induced warming in Europe is a northward shift of the limit at which current temperature is barely sufficient for maturation of crops (Carter et al 1991b). Figure 4.2 illustrates the shift in location of the limits of one crop (grain maize) over a range of time for a high level of warming (the GISS scenario A).

Figure 4.3 illustrates the range in the estimates of shifts, mapping the minimum and maximum extension of crop suitability expected at a given time on the basis of GISS scenarios A and C. This indicates the spatial range of effects of different future emissions rates. Quantifying this, there is a strong likelihood that shifts of sunflower within an area of 1.2 million $km^2$ will occur by the 2030s, but it is possible that an extension within a further area of up to 1.4 million $km^2$ could occur. The corresponding values for soybean are 0.7 and 1.1 million $km^2$, respectively.

Average northward shifts in crop potential of 200–335 km can be expected to occur for each 1°C increase in temperature (Carter et al 1991b). These estimates may vary locally by a factor of two, due to terrain and regional climate; and the rate of shift will depend on the rate of warming. We can be fairly confident that the changes indicated as the lower limits of warming (based

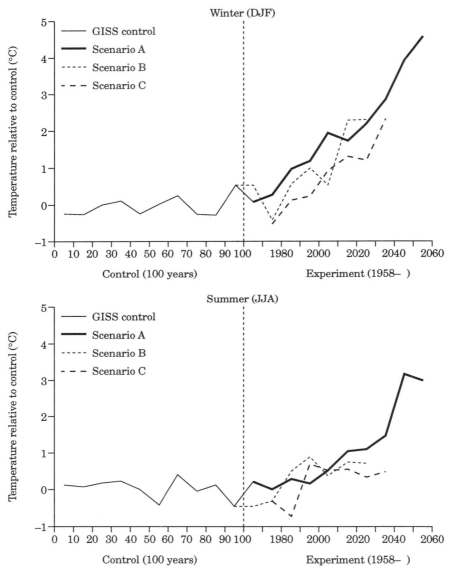

**Figure 4.1** *Decadal mean temperatures projected under the GISS transient-response scenarios A, B and C relative to the control mean for: a) winter, and b) summer in northern Sweden*

Decadal mean temperatures during the 100-year control simulation are also plotted.
Source: Based on data from GISS (Carter et al. 1991b).

on GISS scenario C) will, in most regions, actually occur. There is moderate confidence that GISS scenario B will occur, and low confidence for scenario A. Table 4.1 summarises, for grain maize, and for early-maturing and later-maturing commercial varieties of sunflower and soya, those regions where

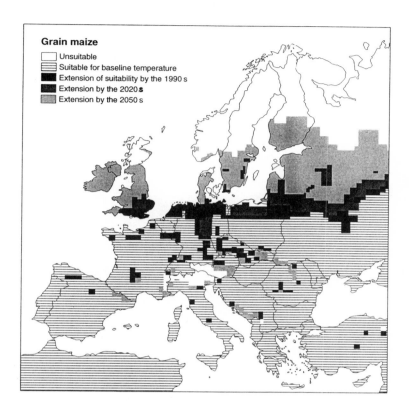

**Figure 4.2** *Shifts in extension of potential grain maize suitability by the 1990s, 2020s and 2050s relative to the baseline under GISS scenario A*

Source: Carter et al 1991b

there is a high, moderate and low likelihood of areas of suitability opening up by two dates in the future: the 2010s and the 2030s. In view of the many other constraints on crop suitability not considered in this assessment, these estimates are necessarily qualitative, and must be regarded as preliminary.

The substantial shifts in crop potential estimated for even the lower-level projections of future temperature change in Europe, represent a significant dislocation of the agricultural resource base relative to present-day conditions. Prima facie, the evidence points to an opening up of new opportunities for crop production in parts of northern Europe but a probable decline of options in areas of southern and eastern Europe, where warming may well be accompanied by reduced moisture availability (Brouwer 1989, Carter et al 1991b)

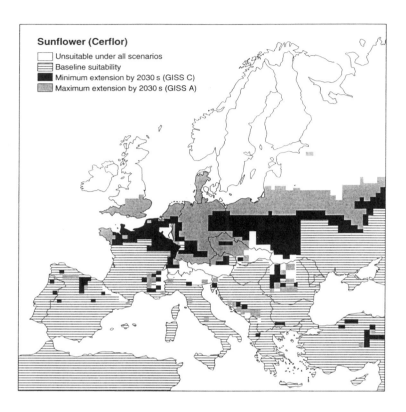

**Figure 4.3a** *Range of estimates of shifts in extension by the 2030s based on GISS scenarios A and C relative to the baseline: early-maturing sunflower (Cerflor)*

Source: Carter et al 1991b

# Effects on Soil Tillage Opportunity

In England and Wales, one of the more pronounced effects of a possible change in climate would be a change in land suitability, defined as the ability of the land to support agricultural activity. This is a crop specific assessment and is broadly classified into four groups ranging from unsuited to well suited. Suitability is calculated on the basis of the relationship between the amount of water available to a growing crop throughout its growth period and the number of good machinery work-days. The number of machinery work-days is calculated for the autumn (1 September to 31 December) and spring (1 January to 31 March) tillage periods. It is determined by estimat-

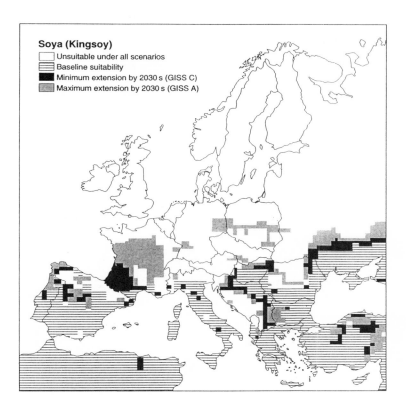

**Figure 4.3b** *Range of estimates of shifts in extension by the 2030s based on GISS scenarios A and C relative to the baseline: later-maturing soya bean (Kingsoy)*

Source: Carter et al 1991b

ing field capacity representing the period over winter when the soil is unable to hold any more water (Thomasson and Jones 1992, Rounsevell and Jones 1993, Rounsevell and Brignall 1994). The field capacity is then compared with a workability assessment which is derived from soil characteristics such as wetness class and retained water capacity (Brignall and Rounsevell 1994).

A major constraint to crop production in England and Wales, especially the wetter north and west, is soil workability and trafficability, both of which are controlled by the weather. Soil conditions for workability are more sensitive to precipitation than temperature because tillage periods occur when precipitation is at its maximum, but evapotranspiration is at a minimum. These results are presented more fully in Rounsevell and Brignall (1994) and Brignall and Rounsevell (1994).

**Table 4.1** *Likelihood of regional temperatures at average altitude being suitable for crop production in the 2010s and 2030s based on GISS scenarios A and C*

| | Likelihood of suitability | | |
| | High | Moderate | Low |
| --- | --- | --- | --- |
| *2010s* | | | |
| Grain maize | S Netherlands | S England | E Denmark |
| | NE Germany | SE Belgium | N Poland |
| | C Czechoslovakia | Luxembourg | Lithuania |
| | N Austria | NW Germany | |
| | NE Poland | N Netherlands | |
| Early sunflower/ soya | C/E Germany | N France | S Netherlands |
| | S Poland | S Germany | Belgium |
| | W Ukraine | | C/W Germany |
| | W Romania | | SW Yugoslavia |
| Late sunflower/ soya | S France | SW France | N Hungary |
| | C Yugoslavia | | |
| | S Ukraine | | |
| *2030s* | | | |
| Grain maize | S England | S Ireland | N Ireland |
| | Benelux | C England | N England |
| | E Denmark | W Denmark | S/C Sweden |
| | N Germany | S Sweden | C Austria |
| | N Poland | Latvia | S Finland |
| | Lithuania | | Estonia |
| | Moscow region | | |
| Early sunflower/ soya | N France | S Netherlands | S England |
| | Belgium | C Germany | E Denmark |
| | W/E Germany | SE England | N Germany |
| | NE Switzerland | | W Czechoslovakia |
| | NE Austria | | N Poland |
| | S Poland | | Lithuania |
| | W Romania | | Moscow region |
| | W Ukraine | | S Sweden |
| Late sunflower/ soya | NW Spain | S/C France | N Portugal |
| | SW France | N Hungary | N/C France |
| | C Yugoslavia | | E/C Germany |
| | C Ukraine | | E Austria |
| | W/E Hungary | | S Poland |
| | | | C Romania |
| | | | W Bulgaria |
| | | | N Ukraine |

Source: Carter et al 1991b

Increases in precipitation tend to decrease the number of work-days regardless of any shift in temperature. However, the magnitude of these effects are dependent totally on geographical location and soil type. Figure

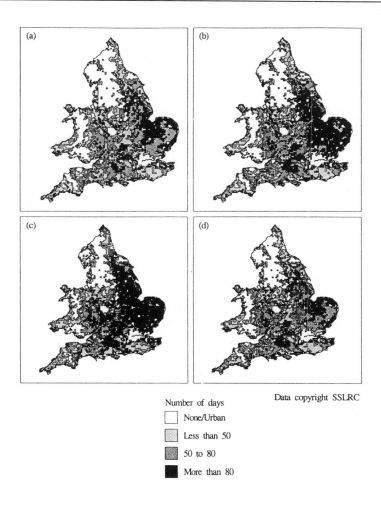

Number of days

☐ None/Urban

▨ Less than 50

▨ 50 to 80

■ More than 80

Data copyright SSLRC

***Figure 4.4*** *Comparison of autumn machinery work-days under changed climates: a) baseline 1961–80, b) temperature +2°C, c) temperature +2°C, precipitation +10 per cent, and d) temperature +2°C, precipitation –10 per cent*

Source: Soil Survey and Land Research Centre, Cranfield University

4.4 compares the effect of a 2°C rise in temperature and a +/–10 per cent change in precipitation on the number of autumn machinery work-days against the current climate. There is a net improvement in soil tillage opportunities, which is greater when the climate is drier. However, large parts of the country do not improve; these regions experience large over-winter precipitation totals. Generally, autumn cultivation requires more than 50 machinery work-days. In the north and north-west of England this occurs in only a few places currently. This pattern is relatively unaffected by either a

2°C rise in temperature or a change in precipitation. In the southwest, by comparison, there are much larger increases in the areas where more than 50 machinery work-days can be expected under a 2°C rise in temperature.

Effects on spring machinery work-days are more difficult to infer. The west of England and Wales shows a similar response to that observed in the autumn, with increasing precipitation resulting in fewer work-days, and increased temperatures resulting in more. However, in the east of the country the number of work-days is determined by whether average annual precipitation is more or less than 650mm. This is because spring machinery work-days are extremely sensitive to spring precipitation and changing the amount of rain can markedly change the end of field capacity date. Moreover, spring precipitation is very variable from year to year. With this amount of inter-annual variability it is unrealistic to consider constant shifts in the baseline conditions because the frequency of good or bad tillage years will have an over-riding influence on the crop potential. Spring machinery work-days may be sufficient *on average* for spring cultivation, but in some years excessive precipitation will inhibit crop establishment. The benefit of higher temperatures and enhanced evapotranspiration appears to have less of an influence on spring machinery work-days than does decreased precipitation.

## Effects on Winter Wheat Potential

The current distribution of winter wheat potential indicates that the best suited land is in south-east, eastern and parts of central England. Fragmented areas of well-suited land also occur in the Welsh Borders. Winter wheat suitability in southeast England is controlled principally by drought stress, whereas in western and northern England and Wales suitability is limited by work-day opportunities (Figure 4.5).

The area of well- and moderately suited land is still largely unaffected when a temperature rise is accompanied by a decrease in precipitation of 10 per cent. Increasing temperature by 2°C causes a change in the percentage area classified well- and moderately suited to 46.4 per cent (Figure 4.5a,b). Increasing precipitation by 10 per cent does little to offset the effects of warming by limiting the increase in well-suited and moderately suited areas to 48.9 per cent with a 2°C rise in temperature (Figure 4.5c).

Increased temperature decreases the amount of moisture available and increases the number of autumn machinery work-days (Rounsevell and Brignall 1994) particularly when associated with a decrease in precipitation. As the increases in work-days and drought assessment vary regionally, there is a shift in the well- and moderately suited areas under altered climate conditions. When precipitation increases, regions limited by drought assessment are favoured, but the much larger loss in work-days associated with this increase is detrimental. This is shown in East Anglia under a 2°C rise in temperature and 10 per cent increase in precipitation, where increased

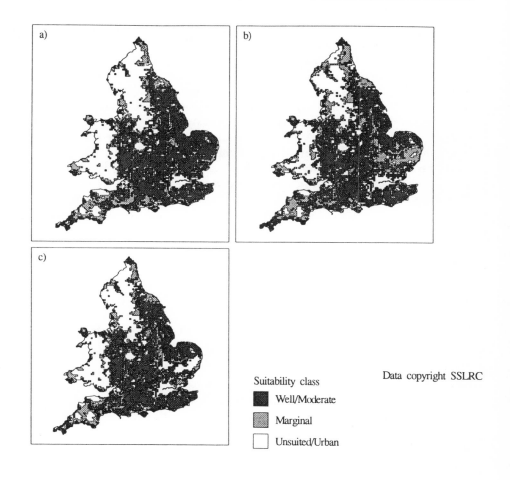

**Figure 4.5** *Winter wheat suitability for: a) baseline climate, b) temperature +2°C and c) temperature +2°C, precipitation –10 per cent*

Source: Soil Survey and Land Research Centre, Cranfield University

precipitation has decreased the number of work-days, thereby making a significant part of the area unsuitable for wheat production (Figure 4.5c).

For autumn-sown cereals such as winter wheat, large moisture deficits leading to severe drought conditions can limit yield (Thomasson and Jones 1992). A future climate that is both warmer and drier would affect yields in south and south-east England. However all responses assume that there is no irrigation. It is currently uneconomic to irrigate winter cereals, but should that change, these regions could experience problems with water resources.

Tillage conditions could improve in currently marginal or unsuited northern and western areas, increasing the suitability of the land. However, tillage conditions are strongly controlled by soil moisture levels and precipitation, and future predictions of these variables are uncertain. Changes in field capacity are important for two reasons. Firstly, a delay in return to field capacity will increase the amount of time available for cultivation. This means that autumn-sown crops can be established in more areas with reduced risk of soil damage. Secondly, and of increasing importance, are the potential problems associated with an excessively dry soil. A soil returning to field capacity in January may well have been too dry for spring cultivation and optimal seed germination (Rounsevell and Brignall 1994).

Winter wheat suitability is more sensitive to changes in precipitation than to changes in temperature. More areas are limited in England and Wales because conditions are too wet during the autumn sowing period rather than the growing season. Decreases in precipitation will benefit areas in south-western and central England. When coupled with increased temperature, benefits are also seen in marginal northern England and Wales. The South East and East Anglia suffer under these conditions because of drought. However, the country-wide changes vary greatly from region to region (Brignall and Rounsevell 1994).

# Effects on Climatic Resources for Crop Growth Requirements

Recent work has used crop-climate relationships to determine the range of climatic conditions throughout the year within which various crops produce an economic yield (Davies et al 1994). Accumulated temperature, solar radiation and soil moisture deficit thresholds were set in order to predict the geographic limits of suitability for growing a given crop to a yield sufficient for an economic return. The growth of the crop was divided into appropriate physiological stages such as seedling emergence, full canopy development and maturity for harvest.

In order for the plant to reach each stage of growth successfully, accumulated temperature, soil moisture and energy from solar radiation had to be within the limits derived from experimental study. Semi-physiological models were selected from the literature for each crop (Table 4.2) and run for current climate in England and Wales (1961–80). The growth of the crop was simulated from planting through to maturity, the timing of the different stages in growth being dependent upon the parameter values between which they were run and the crop's response to the climate inputs.

The crop-climate requirements associated with the different stages of crop growth were imposed on the recorded daily maximum/minimum temperature, rainfall, solar radiation and soil moisture deficits at each meteorological station in England and Wales. If growing conditions at a meteorological station were suitable 50 per cent or more of the years between 1961 and 1980, the mean yield at the station was calculated from the model. This was based on the assumptions: 1) that the crop fitted the farming system; and 2) that the lowest acceptable level of probability for satisfactorily growing the crop was one year in two

(Scullion 1993, personal communication). If the probability was less than 50 per cent the yield for the station was taken as zero and was recorded as unsuitable.

*Table 4.2* *Sources for development of semi-physiological crop-climate models*

| Crop | Model |
|------|-------|
| Potatoes | MacKerron and Waister 1985 |
| Maize | Muchow et al 1990 |
| Grass | Dowle and Armstrong 1990 |
| Spring barley | Kvifte 1987 |
| Pears | Browning and Miller 1992 |

To gain confidence in interpolating and explaining the results of 'current' production, the model yields were validated. Data concerning actual crop growth were collated on a regional basis and, for each region, individual point values of both model yields and actual yield were averaged to gain mean values. These were statistically compared by regression analysis. From the accompanying analysis of variance, model performance in accounting for the variation in actual results ($R^2$) and the level of significance with which model yield related to actual yield (100 − Prob>F) were measured. Additional maps of suitability were then produced for climate scenarios of T+2°C P+/−10 per cent disregarding the direct effect of elevated $CO_2$ on growth.

## Forage Maize and Grass

Assuming the lowest economic yield of forage to be 10 t/ha dry matter (Phipps and Pain 1978, Baker et al 1991), Figures 4.6a and 4.7a confirm that the optimum potential yield of forage maize and forage grass is in the west of England and Wales. In general the east is too dry and the north too cold.

The consequence of increased temperature and precipitation (Figures 4.6 and 4.7) is potential for forage maize production moves north and grassland production increases in the hills and uplands. Such an extension of the growing season might allow maize to mature fully in the southern counties thus increasing the potential for grain production.

However, under a scenario of increased temperature and reduced rainfall large areas of east and south-east England would suffer from moisture stress which would offset the benefits of increased temperature (Figures 4.6 and 4.7). Grass production would remain at 'current' levels and the area would be too dry for forage maize production.

## Maincrop Potato

As the thermal requirement of potatoes is not high, all regions of England and

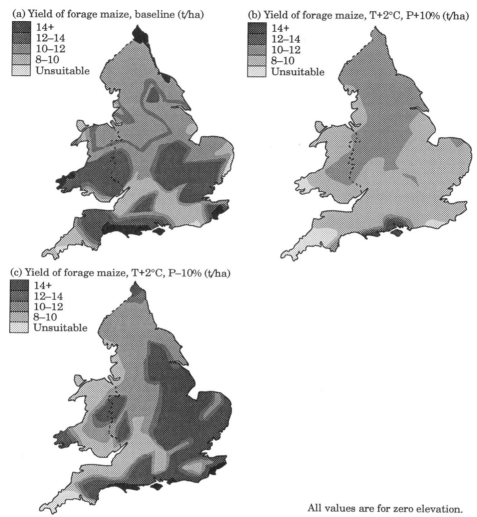

(a) Yield of forage maize, baseline (t/ha)
- 14+
- 12–14
- 10–12
- 8–10
- Unsuitable

(b) Yield of forage maize, T+2°C, P+10% (t/ha)
- 14+
- 12–14
- 10–12
- 8–10
- Unsuitable

(c) Yield of forage maize, T+2°C, P–10% (t/ha)
- 14+
- 12–14
- 10–12
- 8–10
- Unsuitable

All values are for zero elevation.

**Figure 4.6** *Yield of forage maize for: a) baseline, b) temperature +2°C, precipitation +10 per cent and c) temperature +2°C, precipitation –10 per cent*

Wales are suitable for the growth of the crop at >40 t/ha except parts of Cornwall and the estuaries in Wales which are too dry (Figure 4.8). Particularly suitable areas of growth are those receiving more precipitation during the summer months, such as the northern counties of England, parts of the Midlands, the border counties of England and Wales and north Devon around Exmoor. Mountainous regions of Snowdonia, the Cambrians and the Pennines are obviously too cold to support growth. The absence of meteorological stations in these areas prevents these limitations being reflected in Figure 4.8.

Under the scenarios of climate change considered here, yields decrease, particularly in the traditional growth areas of the northern counties. Growth

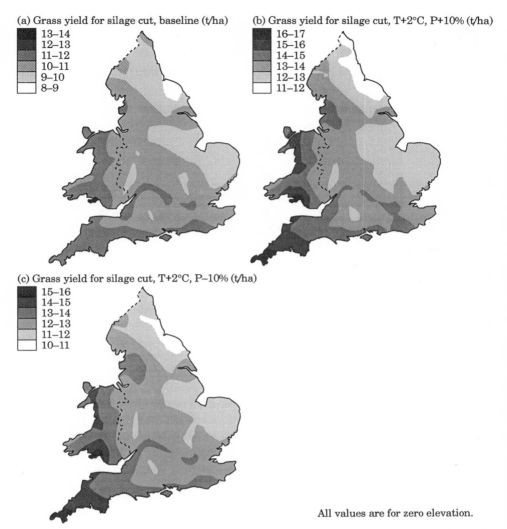

(a) Grass yield for silage cut, baseline (t/ha)

- 13–14
- 12–13
- 11–12
- 10–11
- 9–10
- 8–9

(b) Grass yield for silage cut, T+2°C, P+10% (t/ha)

- 16–17
- 15–16
- 14–15
- 13–14
- 12–13
- 11–12

(c) Grass yield for silage cut, T+2°C, P–10% (t/ha)

- 15–16
- 14–15
- 13–14
- 12–13
- 11–12
- 10–11

All values are for zero elevation.

**Figure 4.7** *Grass yield for silage cut for: a) baseline, b) temperature +2°C, precipitation +10 per cent and c) temperature +2°C, precipitation –10 per cent*

requirements are met less frequently at T+2°C and T+3°C with soil moisture deficits during tuber growth increasing beyond acceptable levels, resulting in lower yields.

# Effects on Land Use in England and Wales

Up to this point we have considered the effects of only those changes of climate occurring over Britain. However, equally important could be the effects of climate changes occurring elsewhere in the world with consequent indi-

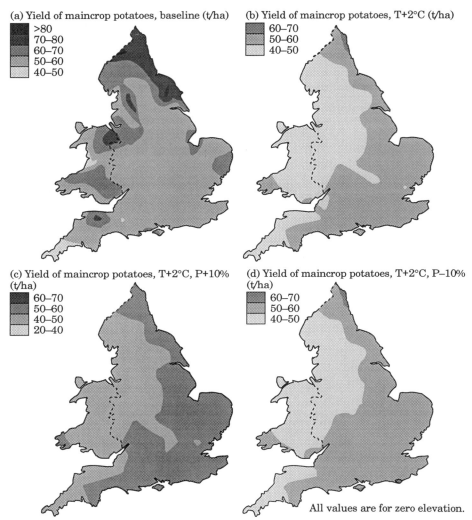

(a) Yield of maincrop potatoes, baseline (t/ha)
- >80
- 70–80
- 60–70
- 50–60
- 40–50

(b) Yield of maincrop potatoes, T+2°C (t/ha)
- 60–70
- 50–60
- 40–50

(c) Yield of maincrop potatoes, T+2°C, P+10% (t/ha)
- 60–70
- 50–60
- 40–50
- 20–40

(d) Yield of maincrop potatoes, T+2°C, P–10% (t/ha)
- 60–70
- 50–60
- 40–50

All values are for zero elevation.

**Figure 4.8** *Yield of maincrop potatoes*

rect effects on British agriculture through the system of world food trade.

A global assessment of the potential effect of climate changes on world food supply suggests that cereal prices may increase due to climate change by 10–25 per cent above those levels predicted for 2060 (in a future without climate change) (Rosenzweig and Parry 1994). The estimated effects on production and prices are given in Figures 4.9 and 4.10. Note that the reference scenarios for 2060 assume United Nations median projections of population (10.3 billion in 2060), economic growth rates based on World Bank projections, technology increases based on Food and Agriculture Organization estimates and a 50 per cent trade liberalisation in agriculture (for example, removal of import restrictions).

The same assumptions, together with the altered prices estimated by the global study, were used as inputs to a climate land use allocation model (CLUAM) of England and Wales to simulate future land use patterns for the reference case (ie without climate change) in 2060. The effect of changes in climate over England and Wales, together with climate-induced changes in world commodity prices were then introduced as experiments with the model (Hossell et al 1994).

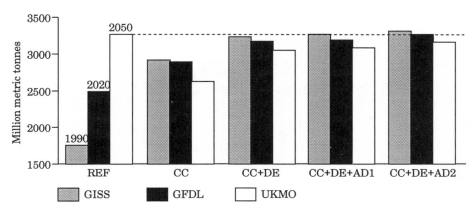

**Figure 4.9** *World cereal production projected for the reference, GISS, GFDL and UKMO doubled $CO_2$ climate change scenarios, with (CC+DE) and without (CC) direct $CO_2$ effects on crop yields, and with adaptation levels 1 and 2 (AD1 and AD2)*

Adaptation level 1 implies minor changes to existing agricultural systems; adaptation level 2 implies major changes.
Source: Rosenzweig and Parry 1994

The model includes nine arable crops and five livestock production systems (Harvey et al 1992), but the results shown here will concentrate on cereals (wheat and barley). Figures 4.11a and b show the distribution of cereals for the 1980s and for the reference case in 2060 (without climate change). These estimations project a loss of cereals area of more than 40 per cent, over the period 1980–2060, due largely to increases in crop yields resulting from technical improvements and reduced trade restrictions. In fact the rate of yield increase used in both the global and CLUAM models is modest (0.48 per cent per year) when compared with the actual rate from 1952 to 1986 (2.2 per cent per year).

A similar reduction in area is seen in all major commodities, with the exception of less intensive operations such as rough grazing and upland leys, which gain land from permanent pasture production. The area of cereals contracts on to land, particularly in East Anglia, that has the greatest comparative advantage in production.

Land use allocations were simulated for the three GCM scenarios considered in the international study (ie GISS, GFDL, UKMO). Only the simulations for the GISS model are shown here (Figure 4.11c). Under this scenario

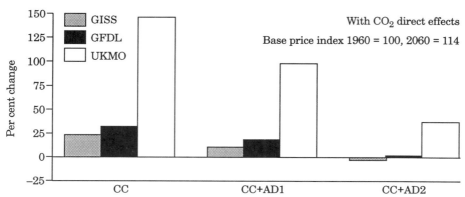

**Figure 4.10** *Change in global cereal prices in 2060 for climate change scenarios (CC), and with adaptation levels 1 and 2 (AD1 and AD2)*

Source: Rosenzweig and Parry 1994

of climate change, which is at the higher end of the IPCC estimate range for warming, the centre of production of cereals moves westward and northward, following the shifts of soil moisture levels due to changes in precipitation. Thus East Anglia becomes less favourable, due to reduced soil moisture, while parts of Lincolnshire and the Vale of York become more favourable.

At present, this analysis of the sensitivity to climate of land allocations in England and Wales is at an early stage. More experiments need to be made to include both other scenarios of climate change and changes in technology and policy.

# Future Patterns

Apart from climate, many other (frequently more influential) factors will also change British agriculture in the future. In the near future, for example, it is envisaged that farming will become less intensive and more environmentally conscious. As a result the landscape will become more species-rich and agriculture more diversified. At present almost 70 per cent of the total agricultural area in Britain and some 90 per cent in Wales, is covered by grassland of one sort or another which is the basis for the ruminant livestock industry. This has accounted for 40–50 per cent of the total agricultural output of Britain in recent years. In the next ten years it is possible that output levels of meat and milk will be capped so that stock numbers are unlikely to expand. Environmental considerations may also play a much greater part in framing government policies which could result in restrictions on current grassland management practices. As a result there might be a move towards alternative animal and crop production. Climate change will thus be one of many factors affecting the opportunities for British farming to move towards alternatives in animal, vegetable, cereal and horticultural production. The face of the British countryside will certainly reflect these changes, just as it has done in the past.

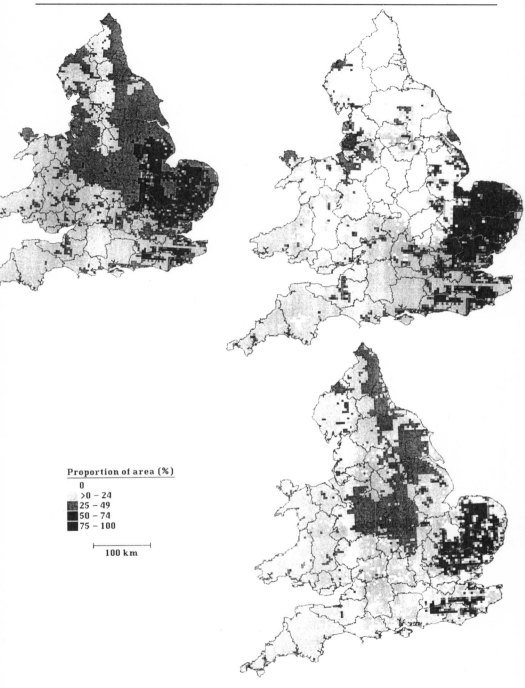

**Figure 4.11** *The distribution of cereals shown by the proportion of agricultural land covered: a) under the mid-1980s optimal run, b) under the REF-2060 run and c) under the GISS 2xCO$_2$ GCM run*

Source: Parry et al, 1996

# 5

# Implications for Energy

---

## Introduction

The energy sector is the key to policies designed to mitigate climate change. More than half of the global emissions of $CO_2$, the most important greenhouse gas, originate in the energy sector. The energy sector is also a significant source of other greenhouse gases, notably methane and nitrous oxides. The Framework Convention on Climate Change signed in 1992 has obliged developed countries to establish policies which aim to stabilise $CO_2$ emissions at their 1990 levels by the year 2000. An intense research effort during the late 1980s and early 1990s has focused on the options for reducing greenhouse gas emissions from the energy sector. The most important options in the short term are the promotion of energy efficiency and switching to fossil fuels, such as natural gas, which emit less $CO_2$ per unit of energy. In the longer term, large-scale development of renewable energy and the expansion of nuclear power have also been advocated.

The immediacy of the policy demands created by the Framework Convention on Climate Change and the potentially significant economic implications for the various actors in the energy sector – consumers, fossil fuel suppliers, renewable energy developers and the nuclear industry – has led to a strong emphasis on the short term with respect to climate change. Measures such as the European Union's proposed carbon/energy tax would have huge economic impacts and could significantly reduce markets for coal and oil. The tax proposal in particular must be seen in the context of wider fiscal reforms designed to address competitiveness and income distribution. One consequence of this intense debate has been that longer-term issues relating to the energy sector have received less attention. The fact that climate change will itself have an impact on the energy sector in the longer term is an issue which has been little addressed. The issue was covered briefly in the first IPCC assessment report (IPCC 1990) and was the subject of a chapter in the first report of the UK Climate Change Impacts Review Group (CCIRG 1991). These review documents show that comparatively little research has been carried out in the area. The research which has been conducted has focused strongly on: a) the impacts of temperature change on energy demand, especially electricity used for space heating and air conditioning; and b) the impacts of water availability on electric power generating systems. A very substantial proportion of the work which has been carried out refers to the United States, while the particular problems which have been addressed are notable chiefly because they are tractable using existing models and methodologies.

There is some debate about how significant climate change will be in the energy sector. Existing energy facilities in France and the United States have certainly been affected by the droughts of the late 1980s. However, a US National Academy of Sciences panel concluded that the energy sector is characterised by a low degree of sensitivity to climate change while the level of adaptability is high (National Academy of Sciences 1992). This conclusion was based on the observation that most energy sector investment will be replaced over the long time-scales associated with climate change, leaving adequate time to adapt. However, one member of the panel dissented from this view, noting that it was the interaction between different economic sectors – water, agriculture, energy, industry – which would determine a society's overall sensitivity to climate change (National Academy of Sciences 1992, p504).

Recognising the relatively small research base, this chapter reviews the possible impacts of climate change on the energy sector in Britain. It begins by considering the types of change which might occur in the energy sector over the next half century. Next, sensitivities to climate change are considered. The remainder of the chapter gives more detailed consideration to the various components of the energy sector – demand, primary energy supply, conventional power generation and renewable energy – and ends by drawing conclusions about the overall sensitivity of the sector, policy implications and areas where there are research needs.

## Energy in the Long Term

Britain is currently dependent on fossil fuels for the bulk of its energy needs. In 1992, oil had the largest market share (35 per cent) followed by coal, in rapid decline (29 per cent), gas (25 per cent), nuclear (8 per cent), imported electricity (2 per cent) and renewables (1 per cent). These shares have changed very significantly over the last 30–40 years (Table 5.1). Coal use has declined consistently, being replaced first by oil during the 1950s and 1960s and then by natural gas during the 1970s and 1980s. Nuclear power has been making steady but unspectacular progress. A further burst of coal-to-gas substitution will take place during the 1990s as existing coal-fired power stations close, to be replaced by combined cycle gas turbine (CCGT) plant. Historically, substitution tends to have taken place through well-defined transitions rather than steady decade-on-decade movements. For example, the market share of natural gas increased very rapidly during the 1970s, but rose only slowly during the 1980s. Such bursts of substitution are likely to take place in the future.

**Table 5.1** *Shares in UK primary energy demand (%)*

|                    | 1960 | 1970 | 1980 | 1990 |
|--------------------|------|------|------|------|
| Coal               | 73.7 | 46.6 | 36.7 | 31.3 |
| Petroleum          | 25.3 | 44.6 | 37.0 | 35.5 |
| Natural gas        | –    | 5.3  | 21.6 | 24.1 |
| Nuclear            | 0.4  | 2.8  | 4.1  | 7.0  |
| Renewables/imports | 0.6  | 0.7  | 0.6  | 2.2  |

Source: Digest of United Kingdom Energy Statistics

Patterns of energy demand have also changed (Table 5.2). Energy demand is no longer increasing as quickly as it did during the 1950s and 1960s. Although there was some growth in the 1980s, the current level of energy consumption is lower than it was in 1973, the peak year for demand. Energy demand from households and 'other consumers' (mainly services and public buildings) has grown modestly, but the main features have been the reduction of industrial energy demand, now 37 per cent below its peak level, and continuing expansion in the transport sector. Here, growth was 3.2 per cent per year during the 1980s.

**Table 5.2** *UK final energy demand by sector (billion therms)*

|              | 1960 | 1970 | 1980 | 1990 |
|--------------|------|------|------|------|
| Household    | 14.4 | 14.6 | 15.8 | 16.1 |
| Industry     | 21.4 | 24.7 | 19.1 | 16.2 |
| Transport    | 8.8  | 11.2 | 14.1 | 19.3 |
| Other users  | 5.9  | 7.4  | 7.5  | 7.7  |
| *Total*      | *50.5* | *58.0* | *56.5* | *59.4* |

Source: Digest of United Kingdom Energy Statistics

The future of the energy sector is very hard to predict and past forecasting exercises have not had auspicious success. Recent scenarios published by the Department of Trade and Industry were constructed on the basis of business-as-usual policy using a variety of economic assumptions (Department of Trade and Industry 1992). The results have been used as a 'reference case' in Britain's climate change programme and are not compatible with $CO_2$ policy objectives (Department of the Environment 1994).

The structure of the British energy sector over the time-scales of climate change is highly uncertain. As Table 5.3 shows, very few physical assets in the energy sector have lives longer than 20 years. Important exceptions are houses and other buildings and major infrastructure such as transportation routes, sites of industrial activity and large-scale projects such as tidal barrages. However, even in buildings, sub-systems such as boilers and central heating systems may be replaced more frequently. Consequently, by the time climate change begins to take effect, say over the period 2020–50, most of Britain's energy infrastructure will have been replaced, some of it several times. With much of the British energy sector having been privatised over the last ten years, the anticipated *economic* lifetime of many types of asset have shrunk considerably. While the former Central Electricity Generating Board used lifetimes of 40 years or so to depreciate power stations, new plants are being depreciated over as little as 15 years, reflecting perceptions of market risk, financial conditions set by lenders and the availability of fuel contracts.

**Table 5.3** *Asset lifetimes in the UK energy sector*

| Asset | Lifetime |
|---|---|
| Conventional light bulb | weeks up to 3 years |
| Electric white goods | 5–10 years |
| Central heating boilers/systems | 10–15 years |
| Motor vehicles | 10–15 years |
| North Sea oil field | 10–30 years |
| Gas supply contract for combined cycle gas turbine | 15 years |
| Renewable energy project | 20 years |
| Conventional power plant | 40–45 years |
| Housing stock | 50 years, but some very long |
| Infrastructure (wayleaves/road/rail/ports) | 50–100 years |
| Tidal barrage | 120 years |

Table 5.4 indicates approximate 'milestone' dates in the energy sector. There is unlikely to be any failure to adapt in the energy sector to climate change and many of the necessary changes can be made 'autonomously' by individual economic agents, as long as they have adequate information on projected climate changes. However, the cost and availability of various energy sources and the design of energy-using equipment may well be affected.

Future developments in the energy sector will be driven by a mixture of underlying economic and resource constraints coupled with policy interventions. While it is impossible to anticipate policy changes over the next fifty years or so, some of the economic/resource considerations are a little clearer. The following points can be used as a basis for considering climate sensitivity:

- ample supplies of fossil fuels are available globally at relatively low cost (World Energy Council 1993). Environmental considerations, including climate change, are likely to be the main constraint on their development;
- energy demand pressures are likely to come from transport fuels and electricity used in homes and offices;
- energy efficiency will continue to improve and, even without policy

interventions, energy demand will increase relatively slowly. Proactive energy efficiency policies could lead to overall declines in demand;

- the potential for using renewable energy is large but it will require public intervention to secure a significant contribution over the coming decades. The Department of Trade and Industry's Renewable Energy Advisory Group considers that a 20 per cent contribution to electricity demand could be achieved by 2025 'under severe pressures of need and economics';
- the biggest uncertainty lies with nuclear power which would need very significant levels of public policy support to overcome high costs and public concerns about safety and waste disposal.

***Table 5.4*** *Timeline for the UK energy sector*

| Date | Event |
| --- | --- |
| 1998 | Non-fossil fuel obligation ends for nuclear power |
| 1998 | Full retail competition in gas and electricity |
| 2000 | $CO_2$ emissions returned to 1990 levels |
| 2005 | Last Magnox nuclear reactor retires |
| 2007 | Life of proven and probable North Sea oil reserves at current production levels |
| 2010 | British sulphur dioxide emissions to decline by 80 per cent |
| 2010 | Last 'dirty' conventional power station closes |
| 2018 | Life of proven and probable North Sea gas reserves at current production levels |
| 2020 | Last conventional power station (Drax) closes |
| 2020 | Last advanced gas-cooled nuclear reactor closes |
| 2025 | Renewables could supply 20 per cent of electricity demand 'under severe pressures of need and economics' |
| 2030 | British energy demand could halve on the basis of a 2 per cent annual reduction |
| 2040 | Sizewell 'B' PWR nuclear station closes |
| 2050 | Life of North Sea oil and gas resources at current levels of production assuming all possible and undiscovered reserves are recoverable |
| 2065 | British energy demand could halve on the basis of a 1 per cent annual reduction |
| 2090 | Full decommissioning of existing nuclear sites begins |
| 2120 | Severn tidal barrage would reach end of design life |

# Climate Sensitivities

The energy sector comprises a wide range of activities and it is therefore sensitive to many climate variables apart from temperature. Table 5.5 summarises the sensitivities of specific components of the British energy sector. Analysing the potential impacts of climate is made difficult because it is not easy to predict even the *direction* of change of many of the secondary variables, particularly at the regional as opposed to the global level. It is reasonably clear that, in Britain, both temperature and sea level will rise. It is anticipated that precipitation will increase in winter and perhaps decline in summer, with a small net increase over the year (see Chapter 1, this volume). However, not all GCMs predict this outcome. There is some consensus that windiness and storminess are also likely to increase. Nevertheless, it is still not possible to carry out a comprehensive and internally consistent assessment of the economic impacts of climate change on the British energy sector based on any specific climate or socio-economic scenario. Quite apart from the wide range of uncertainty associated with such scenarios, the micro-level analysis required to inform such work does not always exist. In most areas it is possible to do no more than identify climate sensitivities.

**Table 5.5** *Climate sensitivities in the UK energy sector*

| | Temperature | Precipitation | Humidity | Wind | Insolation | Storminess | Water availability | Sea-level rise |
|---|---|---|---|---|---|---|---|---|
| *Primary energy* | | | | | | | | |
| Oil/gas production | | | | | | X | | X |
| Coal mining | | X | | | | | | |
| Renewables | X | X | X | X | X | X | X | X |
| *Energy conversion* | | | | | | | | |
| Conventional power | X | | | | | | X | X |
| Petroleum refining | | | | | | | | X |
| *Transmission/transport* | | | | | | | | |
| Pipelines | X | | | | | | | |
| Power cables | X | | | | | X | | |
| *Energy demand* | | | | | | | | |
| Space heating | X | | | X | X | | | |
| Air conditioning | X | | X | | X | | | |
| Agriculture | X | | | | | | X | |

Renewable energy sources are most sensitive to climate change because they are most directly related to physical conditions. However, renewables comprise a very varied set of technologies and each has a distinct sensitivity to climate conditions. Energy suppliers, particularly those in the network industries, gas and electricity, currently have many tools which can be used to predict the impacts of weather conditions on energy demand. Consequently, the sensitivity of energy demand to climate is relatively easy to analyse. Space heating demand is relatively predictable but there are significant uncertainties about the impact of climate change on air conditioning, particularly in temperate climates such as those of Britain. For conventional energy supply, the impacts of climate change are likely to be of the 'nuisance' nature, requiring changes in practice but few identifiable costs.

# Energy Demand

## Overview

The two most climate-sensitive energy uses are space heating and air conditioning (Table 5.6). Space heating is a very significant energy use, accounting for some 30 per cent of final UK energy demand (Hardcastle 1984). Air conditioning is currently a very small energy user, but it is increasing rapidly in importance in commercial buildings. Energy use for air conditioning could be significantly affected by climate change. Other minor impacts are likely to come in the areas of: irrigation pumping in agriculture, refrigeration, and lighting. In most demand sectors, rates of change resulting from climate are likely to be smaller than those which have been experienced in the past due to demand and also smaller than future rates of change which will result from changing socio-economic structures and policy interventions. A possible exception is air conditioning where the level of uncertainty is high.

**Table 5.6** *UK energy demand and climate impacts*

| End use | 1988 demand (PJ) | Per cent of total | Likely change |
|---|---|---|---|
| Space heating | 1986 | 30 | less |
| Air conditioning | 24 | 0.4 | more |
| Refrigeration | 97 | 2 | more |
| Lighting | 144 | 2 | ? |
| Irrigation | tiny | – | more? |
| Transport | 1918 | 31 | – |
| Industrial processes | 1234 | 20 | – |
| Other uses[a] | 963 | 15 | – |

[a] *water heating, cooking, appliances, motive power*
Source: UK Climate Change Impacts Review Group 1991

## Space Heating

Energy demand for space heating is determined primarily by ambient temperature although wind conditions and solar insolation also play a role. Natural gas meets approximately two-thirds of current energy needs for space heating in Britain, with the remainder coming from coal, oil and electricity. The dominance of natural gas is even more pronounced in household heating. Variability in temperature from one year to another significantly affects annual levels of gas demand. Several recent winter heating seasons have been exceptionally warm when measured against a baseline climate defined by average conditions over the period 1950–80. In several years since the mid-1980s, winter temperatures have been significantly higher than those expected under 'normal' climate conditions. In 1989/90, gas send-out was 1.4 billion therms less than might have been expected in an average year, corresponding to some 7 per cent of normal sales. The probability of this occurring, based on a statistical analysis of historic gas sales and weather conditions, was less than 1 in 500. In winter 1987/88, a gas send-out corresponding to a 1-in-100 year was experienced, resulting in a 5 per cent decline in sales (British Gas plc 1992).

The sensitivity of energy demand to weather conditions has been studied extensively by suppliers using statistical analyses of demand patterns. In the electricity sector, it has been necessary to conduct even more detailed analyses relating demand to a variety of climate variables, including cloudiness, precipitation and wind (Parry and Read 1988). This is because electricity cannot be stored and it is desirable to make accurate short-term demand forecasts in order to schedule plant availabilities.

At the level of individual buildings, space heating demand is closely correlated to 'degree-days'. These are the number of days when mean daily temperatures fall below a base temperature of 15.5°C. This is judged to be the level at which space heating is required to maintain occupant comfort after allowing for incidental heat gains. Existing degree-day statistics can be manipulated to project the extent to which energy demand for space heating would be altered by changes in climate. Columns (2) – (4) of Table 5.7 show the relative change in energy demand with respect to current climate in several energy-consuming sectors for the years 2010, 2030 and 2050. The ranges indicated reflect temperature increases of 0.3–1.1°C by 2010, 0.7–2.0°C by 2030 and 1.3–2.9°C by 2050. Current IPCC projections lie in the bottom to the middle of these ranges. Under these conditions, and assuming an unchanged energy demand structure, total energy demand could be depressed by 1–2 per cent by 2010, 3–7 per cent by 2030 and 5–10 per cent by 2050. The effect on energy demand would be most pronounced in the household and service sectors where space heating is the most important end use. Here, a relative reduction in demand of 11–22 per cent appears possible.

The degree-day method implicitly assumes that occupiers do not adjust comfort levels in response to changed climatic conditions. In practice, there is considerable evidence that many occupiers cannot afford to maintain their homes at the temperatures which they might desire. As a result, when temperatures rise, internal comfort levels are adjusted and the decrease in energy demand is less than proportional to the change in degree-days. This behavioural factor is picked up in statistical analyses which relate energy demand to temperature conditions. Feeding the climate-change scenarios described above for the years 2010, 2030 and 2050 into statistical models developed and used by the Department of Trade and Industry (Department of Energy 1989) results in the projected changes in energy demand shown in

**Table 5.7** *Possible impacts of climate change on UK final energy demand (reductions attributable to space heating) (%)*

|  | Degree-day method | | | Statistical method | | |
|---|---|---|---|---|---|---|
|  | 2010 (2) | 2030 (3) | 2050 (4) | 2010 (5) | 2030 (6) | 2050 (7) |
| Household | 3–9 | 7–16 | 11–22 | 4–6 | 5–9 | 7–11 |
| Services | 3–8 | 7–15 | 11–21 | 5–8 | 7–12 | 9–15 |
| Iron & steel | <1 | <1 | <1 | – | – | – |
| Other industry | 1–3 | 2–4 | 3–6 | 1–2 | 2–3 | 2–4 |
| Agriculture | – | – | – | – | – | – |
| Transport | – | – | – | – | – | – |
| *Total* | *1–4* | *3–7* | *5–10* | *2–3* | *3–5* | *4–6* |

Source: UK Climate Change Impacts Review Group 1991

columns (5) – (7) of Table 5.7. As expected, these are less than the changes projected using the degree-day method. However, they are sufficiently similar to give some confidence that the results are robust. In the short term, the changes calculated using statistical techniques are probably more reliable. However, in the longer term, the design of the building stock may change to reflect changed climate conditions (see below) and, as higher standards of comfort are achieved, the degree-day method may begin to reflect climate sensitivities more accurately.

If temperature variability does not change, annual energy demand for space heating will decline more than peak demand, reflecting a shorter heating season. This will result in a lower degree of utilisation of space heating equipment. In principle, this could influence the choice of fuel, for example gas versus electricity. However, this would happen only in the long term and the possibility is speculative.

## Air Conditioning

The utilisation of existing air conditioning systems would be significantly affected by a change of climate. Air conditioning is affected by temperature, humidity and solar heat gain. It is more difficult to correlate the energy demand for air conditioning systems with cooling degree-days (which are conventionally measured from an 18°C base) because of the important role played by humidity and the variability of internal heat gains from one building to another. The adoption of information technology during the 1980s greatly added to internal heat gains in office buildings. Britain's current climate is marginal with respect to air conditioning use and small rises in temperature could lead to a sharp increase in cooling degree-days. Work carried out at the Building Research Establishment indicates that a temperature rise of 4.5°C, considerably higher than that projected by IPCC, would double the average 'full-load' usage of a typical system to 2500 hours per year and would reduce the refrigeration efficiency of the system by 10 per cent (Milbank 1989). It has been estimated that a doubling of electricity demand for air conditioning systems could more than offset temperature-driven reductions in electricity use for space heating systems (CCIRG 1991).

Air conditioning is an almost automatic choice for new office buildings, especially those located in London and the South East or in noisy or polluted urban areas. There was a significant growth in the use of air conditioning associated with the commercial building boom of the 1980s and energy demand in such systems is estimated to have trebled between 1975 and 1985. Over a quarter of office area is now air conditioned (Herring et al 1988). On the other hand, markets for single-unit room air conditioners of the type which are common in the United States, Japan or in parts of Europe have not developed. These can be used either in commercial buildings or in houses. Climate change could encourage a market for such units, but the evidence is limited. A Japanese study found that the *sale* (as opposed to the use) of air-conditioners was correlated with cooling degrees calculated using a baseline temperature of 30°C: 40,000 extra air conditioning units were sold for every degree-day in excess of that temperature (Sakai 1988). It is difficult to extrapolate this result from Japanese to British conditions, but it does suggest that markets for room air conditioners could develop. However, there are simpler and cheaper alternatives available to building occupiers, including shading windows and 'retreating' to cooler parts of the building. In southern Europe, a combination of natural ventilation and window shading is sufficient to ensure adequate comfort levels.

## Building Design and Energy Use

Central heating and air conditioning are common add-on technical fixes to the problem of buildings which do not, by themselves, meet the comfort needs of occupiers. There is a growing interest among architects in 'passive' building design which will lower the need for active heating/cooling systems. This interest is partly driven by concerns about the environmental impacts of such systems in terms of energy use and the use of materials such as chlorofluorocarbons (CFCs). Improved designs could lower space heating demand by taking advantage of solar heat gains ('passive solar') and through higher standards of insulation. Especially in offices, 'intelligent' buildings, making use of window shading and controlled ventilation, perhaps controlled by electronic management systems, could reduce cooling loads.

## Other Uses

The efficiency of refrigeration equipment would be reduced by higher ambient temperatures. However, refrigeration accounts for a very small proportion of British electricity demand. Lighting accounts for about 15 per cent of electricity demand and could be affected by changes in cloudiness and precipitation. However, the nature of these changes is not clear and electricity demand for lighting could decline if high-efficiency luminaires achieve a high market penetration as a result of energy efficiency policies.

Electricity use in agriculture represents only 0.2 per cent of final energy demand in Britain and any climate impacts would have little overall economic significance. However, electricity accounts for 65 per cent of farmers' expenditure on energy. A US study concluded that electricity demand for irrigation pumping is sensitive to temperature rather than precipitation (Wolock et al 1992) and that a 0.6–0.9°C temperature rise would increase energy demand by around 25 per cent (Darmstadter 1991). However, irrigation accounts for only a proportion of electricity demand and the US study found that the increase in electricity costs in agriculture would not exceed 3 per cent.

## Implications for Energy Supply Investment

Changes in patterns of energy demand will feed through into investment in energy supply. The impact of climate change on *peak* demand rather than *total annual* demand will be the critical factor. For fossil fuels, which are used for space heating, peak demand requirements will decline, reducing the need for new investment in supply capacity and pipelines. For electricity, the position is less clear. Total annual demand for electricity could rise as a result of climate change because of increased demand from air-conditioners, but the peak demand, which occurs in winter, could fall as a result of reduced space heating needs. In some parts of the world, including much of the United States and southern Japan, peak demand occurs in summer, primarily because of the use of air conditioning systems. In 1993/94 in England and Wales, the peak demand in winter (December to February) was 46.9 GW while peak demand in summer (June to August) was only 35.7 GW (NGC Settlement Systems 1993, 1994). A very substantial rise in energy demand for air conditioning would be required to induce an 11 GW increase in summer load and a consequent switch to a summer-peaking regime. This does not seem likely, although more research is required to understand better the factors determining air conditioning energy demand and the potential extra load.

Climate induced changes in electricity demand could delay very slightly the need to invest in new generating capacity and will influence the type of plant chosen. In principle, higher load factors will favour plant with lower operating costs and higher capital costs which will, in turn, have small subsequent impacts on electricity prices. However, climate impacts will be felt over very long time-scales and they are likely to be small in comparison to market- or policy-driven changes.

# Fossil Fuel Supply

## Oil and Gas Production

Britain is an important producer of oil and gas and is currently self-sufficient in oil. Small amounts of natural gas are imported. As production of North Sea oil and gas runs down during the 21st century, self-sufficiency is unlikely to continue. Oil and gas production is located off-shore and is carried out under demanding conditions which makes it potentially sensitive to changed climate. The key variables are sea-level rise and storm activity. Major oil companies have taken note of the potential impacts of climate change on offshore operations but little is available in the public domain. Shell has increased the height of its North Sea gas platforms by 1–2m above the water level to take account of projected sea-level rise over the lifetime of the installations (National Academy of Sciences 1992, p606). However, the total cost of a platform will be raised by less than 1 per cent as a result of this measure.

Climate change could lead to higher waves and more frequent storms. In the Canadian Beaufort Sea, it has been projected that the frequency of occurrence of six metre waves would rise from 16 per cent to 39 per cent. This would have a negative impact on the offshore oil and gas industry in that the design requirements for both offshore structures and associated coastal facilities would be increased (McGillivray et al 1993). In addition, the number of periods in which supply vessels and helicopters would be unable to operate would be increased.

The international oil and gas industry now works under even more demanding climate conditions than those found in the North Sea, for example in the Canadian Arctic and Siberia. Therefore, the industry would be able to adapt to more demanding climate conditions. In any event, North Sea oil and gas production will run down during the next few decades as reserves are depleted.

## Coal Mining

Underground coal mining is in rapid decline in Britain and would, in any event, be relatively insensitive to climate change. Open-cast mining operations would be affected by higher levels of rainfall in winter leading to an increased frequency of flooding and potential pollution problems. Conversely, longer drier summers could make it harder to suppress dust at stockpiles held at both mines and consumers' premises. Coal preparation requires considerable quantities of water and an increased frequency of droughts could curtail production and push up costs (CCIRG 1991). These impacts are of the nature of 'nuisances' rather than major threats to activity. It is not clear whether there will be a coal industry in Britain by the middle of next century.

# Renewable Energy

## Overview

Supported by the non-fossil fuel obligation (NFFO) established under the 1989 Electricity Act, the amount of renewable energy produced in Britain is set to grow rapidly. However, renewables still account for only 6 TWh of electricity generated in Britain out of a total generation of 326 TWh (Department of Trade and Industry 1993a, Table 48). It has been established that the potential for renewable energy generation in Britain is as much as 60 TWh per year by the year 2025 (Department of Trade and Industry 1994). Table 5.8 shows the 'possible contributions' of various forms of renewable energy in Britain by the years 2005 and 2025. The lower range for 2025 (15–60 TWh) in the final row of the table is the United Kingdom Renewable Energy Advisory Group's 'plausible estimate' of what is feasible under 'severe pressures of need and economics'.

***Table 5.8*** *Possible contributions of renewable energy in the UK*

| Source | Possible contribution by 2005 (TWh/year) | Possible contribution by 2025 (TWh/year) | Capacity contracted in first NFFO tranches (MW) |
|---|---|---|---|
| Wind | up to 30 | up to 30 | 53 |
| Hydro | 4.2–6.2 | 4.2–6.2 | 19 |
| Tidal | – | – | |
| Wave | up to 0.16 | up to 0.16 | |
| Photovoltaics | up to 0.03 | up to 7.2 | |
| Solar thermal | up to 0.01 | up to 2.5 | |
| Geothermal | – | – | |
| Waste incineration | 0.92–6.1 | 0.4–10 | 72 |
| Landfill gas | 0.27–7.7 | up to 6.3 | 74 |
| Agricultural wastes | 0.034–5.2 | up to 6.5 | |
| Energy crops | up to 21 | up to 150 | |
| Sewage gas | | | 33 |
| *Total* | *15–75* | *15–190* *(15–60)* | *251* |

Source: Department of Trade and Industry 1994

Over the timescales associated with climate change, renewable energy could make a significant contribution to meeting British primary energy needs. Climate sensitivity is worth considering because most forms of renewable energy are directly dependent on climatic resources. Much of the renewable energy supported under the first two tranches of the NFFO is associated with landfill gas and waste incineration. These stretch the definition of renewable energy and they show little climate sensitivity. This section focuses on wind, energy crops, ocean energy systems (tidal and wave power) and solar. Between them, wind and energy crops account for over 80 per cent of the possible renewable contribution by the year 2025.

## Wind

So far, 29 wind energy projects have been stimulated by the NFFO and the long-term potential is considerable. The wind regime in Britain is very favourable. Climate change could affect: a) the quantity of the wind resource available; and b) the operation and design of wind turbines. The energy flux associated with wind varies with the cube of the wind velocity (Cavallo et al 1993). The capacity of any wind turbine is therefore very sensitive to wind-speed. It has been postulated that average windspeeds will increase under climate change because the temperature gradient between the poles and the equator, which drives the wind system, will increase (Grubb and Meyer 1993). There are no reliable projections of windspeeds under climate change. However, it has been observed that there are 7200 km$^2$ of land in Britain with average windspeeds above 8m/s and a further 4500 km$^2$ with wind-speeds above 7.7m/s (Chester 1988). Even a small increase in windspeed would therefore expand the potential resource considerably.

Wind turbines are vulnerable to climate impacts in a number of ways:

* high windspeeds can cause turbines to fail;
* severe weather, including storms, snow and ice, can cause significant damage to machines – the incidence of storms could increase, while that of snow and ice could decline;
* fouling of turbine blades by insects and dust under dry summer conditions can reduce energy output.

If wind turbines are designed with these factors in mind, no significant climate-related problems should be encountered. Wind turbines have a design life of less than 20 years (Hillsman and Petrich 1994) and climate should not change significantly over the life of any specific machine.

## Energy Crops

The use of energy crops to generate electricity is still at the research and development stage in Britain. However, some demonstration projects are likely to be supported in the third NFFO tranche. The potential for energy crops is greater than that of any other renewable energy source. The most likely route in Britain is the coppicing of high-yield willow and poplar trees, with harvested wood being gasified and burned in advanced generation plants (Department of Trade and Industry 1994). The availability of land could be the greatest constraint on this energy source. Set-aside policies may encourage the use of land for non-food crops. The production of ethanol as a transport fuel derived from cereal crops is also a possibility.

The cost and availability of energy crops will be influenced by climate variables in the same way as other forestry or agricultural products. Tree growth may be enhanced by increased $CO_2$ concentrations though this depends on there being fertile land and an adequate supply of water (Fajer and Bassaz 1992). It is not yet clear whether increased $CO_2$ concentrations yield more than short-term benefits. Extreme events such as storms, pests and frosts can all have an adverse effect on trees. Coppiced stands grown in a European situation appear to be relatively resistant to storms.

## Tidal and Wave Power

The technical potential for tidal energy in Britain is considerable, but the economics are not promising. Tidal barrages, such as those proposed for the Severn, are highly capital intensive and would involve long lead-times. For that reason, the Renewable Energy Advisory Group does not foresee the development of such projects in the coming decades. Barrages would have a very long design life, of the order of 120 years, and it would be essential to take account of changes in sea level and any increase in storm activity which might take place over this time-scale.

There have been a considerable number of wave energy research and development projects carried out worldwide, but it is does not appear that this technology will lead to competitive electricity generation in the short-to-medium term. If wave energy were developed, sea-level rise and changes in storm activity would necessarily have to be taken into account (Department of Trade and Industry 1994).

## Solar

Britain's latitude and climate limit the potential for solar energy. Solar thermal systems, used for heating purposes, rely on direct sunlight to heat water. The potential energy from such systems is limited by cloud cover and they would need to be backed up by more conventional heating methods. Solar thermal potential is affected in minor ways by wind, dust and storm activity.

Photovoltaic devices for generating electricity may be slightly more promising because flat-plate devices rely on diffuse light scattered by clouds as well as on direct sunlight. In Britain, integrating photovoltaic technology into the roofs of suitable buildings might be the best option, though the costs could be high (Department of Trade and Industry 1994). The conversion efficiency of photovoltaic cells falls with temperature, but this is unlikely to be a problem in Britain. Photovoltaic cells generate direct current which must be transformed into alternating current before being fed into a grid system. The electronic components which do so are highly vulnerable to moisture and overheating. The structures used to support photovoltaic cells are vulnerable to high windspeeds.

# Energy Conversion

## Coastal Siting

Many energy supply and conversion activities are located on coasts and estuaries, including offshore oil and gas service facilities, petroleum refineries and conventional (coal, oil and nuclear) power stations. These are all potentially vulnerable to sea-level rise and increased levels of storm activity. All 14 of Britain's oil refineries are located on the coast so as to facilitate access to supplies of sea-borne crude oil. Re-location of these plants is highly unlikely because of the huge economic advantages conferred by coastal siting and because most are connected to the existing products' pipeline network. The need for additional protection against sea-level rise will be very site-specific and no generic assessment is possible. Changes in markets for refined petroleum products and tighter environmental controls are much more likely than climate change to affect refinery closure or re-location.

Most of Britain's conventional power stations are located on the coast so as to provide ready access to cooling water and/or to facilitate the supply of coal or fuel oil. All currently operating nuclear power stations are located on the coast. In the future, fossil fuel power stations will become less dependent on cooling water as steam-based systems are replaced by gas turbines. In CCGT plant of the type which is currently being installed in the electricity supply industry, two-thirds of the electricity is generated by gas turbines and the residual by steam turbines. As with petroleum refining, the potential vulnerability of existing power stations is very site-dependent. Closure or re-location as a result of climate change is unlikely.

It is less clear whether climate will affect the siting of future facilities. CCGTs are less dependent on cooling water than are existing coal- and oil-fired stations. Even if coal becomes the chosen fuel for new power stations in the early decades of next century, advanced technologies such as integrated gasification combined cycle (IGCC) are less dependent on cooling water. There are still good reasons to locate new coal stations on the coast to provide easy access to coal imports. All potential sites for new nuclear stations are also located on the coast. Power station sites tend to be used for long periods and more than one vintage of plant may be built at the same site in order to take advantage of connections to the transmission network and existing planning consents. In general, there is a strong inertia associated with energy conversion facilities such as refineries and power stations. The inertia is due to past investments in infrastructure facilities such as roads, rail links, ports and transmission lines as well as the obtaining of planning consents. This will tend to mitigate against major re-location of activity. Building-in suitable levels of storm protection from the beginning will be less expensive than modifying established sites.

## Conventional Power Generation

Conventional power generation based on steam turbine technology requires considerable quantities of cooling water in order to condense steam at the end of the cycle. The two options are: a) once-through cooling where water is abstracted and returned to its source at a higher temperature; and b) evaporative cooling where water is 'consumed' through being evaporated to the atmosphere in cooling towers. Power stations sited on rivers or lakes equipped with either type of cooling are sensitive to limited water availability as a result of drought conditions. It may be necessary to curtail power production:

- if river levels fall below the level of the cooling water inlet pipe;
- if, with once-through cooling, thermal pollution becomes excessive in relation to the river flow;
- if, with evaporative cooling, the amount of water consumed becomes excessive in relation to the river flow;
- if, for nuclear plant, there is the possibility of breaching safety limits.

All of these conditions have been met during droughts in France and the United States in recent years (Miller et al 1992). There is considerably less likelihood of these types of events becoming common in Britain. The only nuclear power station which was located on a lake has recently shut. Coal-fired plants which rely on river water for cooling tend to be smaller and older than plant located on coasts or estuaries. Many are being shut under National Power/PowerGen closure programmes.

In the longer run, as mentioned above, new fossil fuel plants such as CCGTs and, possibly, IGCC coal plants will be much less reliant on cooling water. This will not be the case for any new nuclear plants which will continue to use steam turbines. However, nuclear plant would be located on the coast where sea water would be used.

The efficiency of conventional power plants would be reduced slightly because of higher ambient temperatures. The reduction in efficiency would be higher for gas turbines than would be the case for steam turbines. New CCGT plant would be relatively more affected than conventional plant. However, the baseline efficiency of CCGTs is also much higher than that for simple steam plant. CCGTs operate satisfactorily under tropical conditions and higher temperatures should cause no technical problems.

# Transport and the Transmission of Energy

Electricity is transmitted at high voltage in Britain by means of overhead lines while most low voltage distribution lines are buried beneath the ground. Overhead lines are vulnerable to storms and icing. The major storms of 1987 and 1990 caused considerable damage to the electricity transmission system in Britain. During the October 1987 storm, electricity consumers in England and Wales lost an average of 250 minutes supply (Electricity Council 1988). The loss of service was even greater for customers located in the South East. As well as the direct cost of repairing damage, there is an economic cost associated with the loss of supply. This is hard to quantify. However, using the value-of-lost-load benchmark then used by the electricity supply industry to calculate surplus capacity needs, the cost of the 1987 storm to customers would have been £200 million. The value of lost load was fixed at £2/kWh at the time.

Overhead power lines sag as the current passing through them rises and this effect is exacerbated by higher ambient temperatures. This sagging limits the capacity of overhead lines. The thermal capacity of a 400 kV double circuit line in Britain ranges from 2190 MVA in summer to 2720 MVA in winter (Eunson 1988). This corresponds to a temperature range of just over 10°C. Higher temperatures associated with climate change would, therefore, slightly reduce the capacity of the transmission network. The precise impacts would depend on the development of the network. In principle, there could be a need to accelerate the upgrading of existing lines or a need to operate more power stations 'out-of-merit', pushing up generation costs. However, the overall effects are likely to be minor.

Coal, oil and gas are moved by water, road, rail and pipeline. Pressure in gas pipelines is maintained by gas turbine compressor stations. These would have to work slightly harder at higher temperatures, but the impacts would be minor. Winter problems, such as ice and snow, which affect road transport of coal and oil could be eased slightly with climate change but, again, the magnitude of the impacts would be small.

# Conclusions

This chapter supports, at a general level, the conclusion that the energy sector is relatively insensitive to climate change and that the level of adaptability is high. The lifetime of most equipment used on both the supply and the demand side of the market is shorter than the time-scales associated with climate change. In most cases, climate change will require relatively minor technical changes to the design of equipment. These changes could be made by companies and consumers as long as they are well-informed about projected changes in climate. In some respects, on-going technical and economic change in the sector will serve to reduce sensitivity to climate. Reduced dependence on cooling water associated with the move from steam cycles to gas turbines in power generation is one example of this development.

However, there are some exceptions to the general rule which have implications in terms of policy and research:

- possible climate-induced changes in the level of demand for space heating fuels are sufficiently large to be worth while taking into account in defining baseline climates for assessing the need for supply investment;

- there are very considerable uncertainties concerning the future level of electricity demand for air conditioning. This demand could be influenced greatly by climate change and increases in summer temperatures. More research into this issue is warranted;
- the relationship between climatic factors and the potential for renewable energy sources is not yet fully understood. A better understanding would help in the development of renewable energy sources. Wind energy and energy crops would be a priority for this type of work.

# 6

# Implications for Insurance and Finance

## Introduction

The purpose of this chapter is to discuss the type of extreme climatic events which damage the insurance industry and how shifts in these patterns arising from climatic change might affect the whole financial sector. A subsidiary purpose is to consider what role the sector might play in combating climate change. Most of the chapter deals with insurance, because until now the other financial industries, such as banking, have taken very little notice of this issue.

Currently the property insurance subsector bears the brunt of weather impact on the financial sector. The contracts (policies) insure against damage from a weather 'event' which is generally understood as a wide departure from normal conditions (ie an 'extreme').

When an extreme event occurs it has an impact on the insurer in various ways: claims exceed the 'risk premium', operations are disrupted, assets may lose value. If the whole pattern of events becomes extreme, with excessive claims over a prolonged period, this may affect the size of the market, as insurers (and reinsurers) will attempt to raise their prices or restrict the amount of cover they provide. The consumers will in turn react to the new supply situation and their own revised perceptions of risk.

British property insurers are unusually exposed to climatic hazards in two ways. Firstly, they take on risks overseas, where conditions are frequently more extreme than in the domestic market (probably only 60 per cent of property premiums written by British insurers are actually on risks based in Britain). Secondly, standard British household and small traders' policies cover a comprehensive range of hazards, including crime, trade processes and weather. Almost unique to Britain is the inclusion of subsidence, heave, landslip (excluding coastal erosion) and also flood. Traditionally, the main property risk has been fire, followed by theft (Dlugolecki et al 1994). To its credit the government included insurance in its study of the potential impact of climate change in Britain (Dlugolecki 1991).

# The Insurance Industry and Critical Events

## Market Influences

What constitutes a critical event depends upon a wide variety of 'market' or socio-economic factors, not just the weather.

### Demographic changes

Urbanisation remains high in Britain, and this means that when an extreme event occurs, the cost will also be extreme (either very low in sparsely populated areas, or very high for cities). Current statistics suggest that about 70 per cent of the insured loss costs of storms relate to domestic property. This is explained by the sector's greater size, the comprehensive nature of domestic property covers and, in relative terms, the greater vulnerability to damage because of construction materials/methods. The potential domestic sector size continues to increase with the number of dwellings increasing from 16.2 million in 1961 to 23 million in 1991 whilst in the same period the number of owner-occupiers more than doubled.

### Insurable property and the built environment

The value of the damaged property is a key issue. Britain has been plagued by enormous surges in property values, followed by stagnation or even collapse. This makes it difficult for an insurer to assess its liability, because the difference between rebuilding and replacement costs has been reversed. This is important for such strategic considerations as control of the total 'accumulation' of risks, and investment decisions, and also for individual claims where major damage has occurred.

Current statistics suggest that about 70 per cent of the insured loss costs of storms relate to domestic property. This is explained by the sector's greater size, the comprehensive nature of domestic property covers and, in relative terms, the greater vulnerability to damage because of construction materials/methods. Possessions have become more valuable and also more damageable – for example, satellite dishes. The increasing use of water in the home for cleaning and heating is a potential hazard.

During the same period a number of parallel changes have occurred for commercial risks, often with extremely high values being concentrated in quite modest-sized units. Owing to such modern techniques as 'just-in-time' production and the use of highly specialised electronic equipment, claims for business interruption are becoming increasingly expensive.

In many cases over-intense development has effectively covered the ground with concrete. This has dramatically reduced the capability of the ground to absorb precipitation, with a consequent escalation in the rate of run-off leading to localised 'flash' flooding, even in years of drought.

Finally, it is commonplace after disasters to find that much of the damage is due to substandard construction, often due to inadequate training or supervision during building, rather than poor design. The consequences of one structure failing are serious, since wind-blown debris can damage sound structures.

### Covers

Household insurance has gone through a metamorphosis since the last war. Post-war fire and theft cover were sold as separate policies. By the late 1950s household comprehensive policies had begun to appear which, due to competition, have become more 'comprehensive' over time. Flood cover only became widely available in 1961, following agreement between insurers and the government that all householders and small businesses should be able to insure contents against flood damage 'at reasonable rates'. Cover for buildings was also made more generally available (normal extra premium in 1961 was 3d (1.25p) per £100 cover). Currently, 98 per cent of insured householders are covered for flood damage at normal rates, with just 2 per cent having to pay extra. Subsidence and landslip cover was first added to domestic buildings policies in 1971 (at no cost), producing 164 claims in Britain that year. Heave was not included, but was added later as a separate peril. Since 1979 about 10 per cent of household claims cost has related to subsidence damage. Developments like 'new-for-old' replacement, index-linked values, and 'All-Risks' cover have resulted in greater claims costs also.

## The Hazard

In Britain, the critical hazards are inundation and storm, with subsidence running third. These reflect the potential cost, and the damage seen in historical events. Other hazards such as freeze, flash flood and wildfire are unlikely to be critical. Overseas, the continental scale of geography elevates convective storms, snow and freshwater flood well above the intensity seen in Britain.

Figure 6.1 illustrates the cost of storm, flood and freeze to British insurance companies on British risks since 1960. The dominant hazard is clearly storm which has shown an alarming increase recently (total damages were £1250 million in 1987 and £1900 million in 1990). By way of comparison, subsidence due to extreme drought cost about £500 million in 1990. There were no major floods between 1960 and 1992 – the Perth floods in 1993 cost about £25 million and the Chichester floods of 1994, about £40 million.

While these figures give a good indication of trends, there are some drawbacks. They do not include uninsured losses which used to be a larger proportion of all losses than now and which exclude claims due to business interruption or vehicle damage. They relate only to member companies of the Association of British Insurers, which account for about 90 per cent of the British market. The method of collection was haphazard; some events

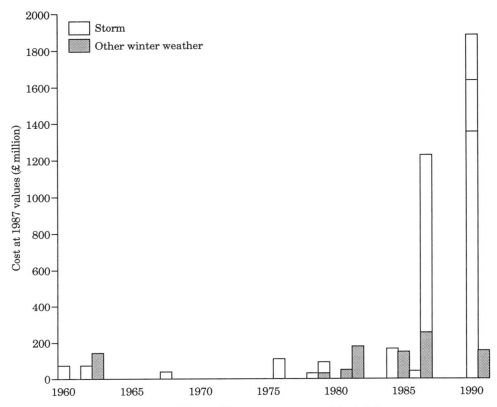

**Figure 6.1** *Major UK winter events 1960–91*

Events as defined by ABI. Costs for 1981/82 and 1990 split by General Accident. Figures exclude non-ABI members and Lloyd's, uninsured losses, motor vehicles and commercial business interruption.
Source: Association of British Insurers

were omitted, while in other cases, the duration and extent of the 'catastrophe' was probably exaggerated. For the freeze of 1981/82, the claims have been apportioned between years on the basis of individual companies' statistics and similarly the 1990 storm costs have been split into three, the two worst events, and 'the rest'. Generally the figures are based on early estimates of the likely cost, provided by experienced claims officials. Only in one case (October 1987) were the figures updated because the initial figure was grossly understated.

For many hazards, their uneven presence and/or the varying nature of insurance involvement around the world makes it difficult to give an international picture. The one peril which does occur everywhere is windstorm, and cover against it is provided in most countries. Table 6.1 contains information on the impact of major windstorms worldwide since 1960. The statistics are based on analyses by major reinsurance companies, and they relate to those storms which cost at least $500 million in 1990 values. To allow a valid comparison for the partial decade of the 1990s, the figures have been expressed as an annual rate. As with Figure 6.1 for British winter losses, there is a very clear upward trend in the number and overall cost. In addition, the proportion of insured damage has risen rapidly from only 25 per cent in the 1960s, to over 50 per cent in the 1990s. The table cuts off in 1992, but in fact there has been at least one 'billion dollar' event in every year since 1987. With computer simulation models, it is possible to calculate the cost of scenarios in which these storms followed different, but credible, tracks. For example, if hurricane 'Andrew' had been 50 miles further north, then the cost could have been three times as great, at $50 billion.

*Table 6.1* Major windstorms worldwide annual impact 1960–92

|                            | 1960s | 1970s | 1980s | 1990s |
| -------------------------- | ----- | ----- | ----- | ----- |
| Number                     | 0.8   | 1.3   | 2.9   | 5.0   |
| Total damage ($ billion)   | 2.0   | 2.9   | 3.4   | 20.2  |
| Insured cost ($ billion)   | 5.0   | 0.8   | 1.7   | 11.3  |

Valued at 1990 prices, 1990s include 1990, 1991 and 1992 only.
A major windstorm is defined as one costing more than $500 million in total damage.
Source: Munich Re and Swiss Re

Experience shows that damage to property responds non-linearly to increasing weather severity. Much work has been done on storm damage severity curves, not so much on the other perils. Figure 6.2 shows the typical response, using data from the October 1987 'hurricane' in Britain. The peak gusts were about 90mph in urban areas, resulting in damage which cost 1 per cent of the property value in the worst-affected areas. To put this in perspective, it should be recalled that the average premium rate for domestic buildings in Britain is about 0.2 per cent, to cover a comprehensive range of perils from fire to accidental damage as well as administration and profit. Research on flood claims in the 1990 Towyn incident shows a similar sharp increase, with the potential cost being very high on individual properties. The critical threshold was a depth of salt water of 5cm, because of the corrosion damage to such services as gas and electricity, as well as appliances (Dlugolecki et al 1994).

# Future Climate Changes and their Impacts

## The Hazard

In order to study the potential effects of greenhouse gas-induced warming on the insurance industry, scenarios of climate change at the regional and subregional scale are required. Excellent reviews of methods of regional scenario development are provided by Cohen (1990) and by Giorgi and Mearns (1991). The best source of information about climate change at the regional

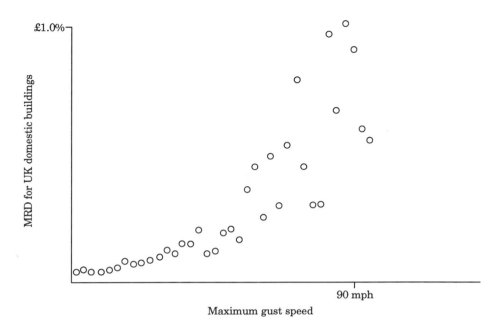

**Figure 6.2** *Storm cost and windspeed (October 1987)*

MRD is based on ABI data at postcode district level of claims cost as a ratio of total value of insured property, for domestic buildings. Windspeed is interpolated from maps in Buller, 1988.

scale is from general circulation models (GCMs): complex, three dimensional, computer-based models of the atmospheric circulation.

Most of the scientific literature on climate change at the regional scale is devoted to the study of the average climate (see for example Boer et al 1992, Grotch and MacGracken 1991, Palutikof et al 1992). These are of limited interest to insurers, whose principal concern is the extreme event. Parry (1978) and Wigley (1985) showed that, if the mean of a normally distributed climate variable changes, while the standard deviation remains constant, then the occurrence of extreme events (defined as events exceeding a specific threshold) will change in a highly non-linear way. As an example, Wigley demonstrated that a reduction in annual mean England and Wales precipitation of 100mm would cause a drought that is expected to occur one year in a hundred to become around 7.5 times more likely. Mearns et al (1984) showed a similar effect in their study of high temperature events in the US Corn Belt. A perturbation of +1.7°C in mean temperature caused the likelihood of a run of five consecutive days with maximum temperatures greater than 35°C to become three times greater.

It is likely that climate changes will affect the variability as well as the mean of a climate variable such as temperature or precipitation. The effect on the occurrence of extreme events of a change in variability is shown in Figure 6.3. The frequency of extreme events changes at both ends of the distribution whereas, with a change in the mean, the frequency increases at one end of the distribution but is accompanied by a decrease at the other end. Katz and Brown (1992) have shown that the frequency of extreme events is relatively more dependent on changes in variability than in the mean. The sensitivity is relatively greater the more extreme the event. They comment that 'experiments using climate models need to be designed to detect changes in climate variability and . . . policy analysts should not rely on scenarios of future climate involving only changes in means'.

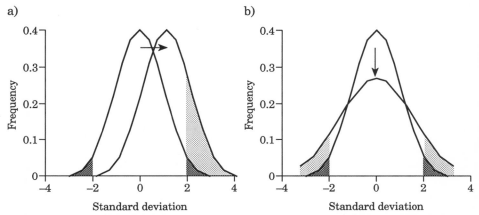

**Figure 6.3** *Effect of a change in a) mean only; b) variability only, on the occurrence of extreme events*

Note: in case a), the incidence of events greater than two standard deviations from the original mean increases only at the upper end of the distribution. In case b), where variability is increased, there is an increase in extreme events at both ends of the distribution. X-axis units apply to the original distribution.
Source: Redrawn from Mitchell et al 1990

Unfortunately, such studies are rare. There are three principal reasons for this. This first is that modelling groups have not always retained the necessary daily model output information. Second, validation at a daily scale generally demonstrates large differences between observations and model output. Scientists have preferred to use model output at the monthly, seasonal or annual scale where, in general, model performance is more reliable. The final reason is that even where daily data are retained, there may be too few for the study of extreme events.

### Studies of climate variability using statistical techniques

Difficulties associated with obtaining long reliable daily time series from GCMs have led to the application of statistical models to generate time series for impacts analysis. Often, these statistical models are in some way initialised with information from GCMs. The simple approach has been to take a daily time series of meteorological observations, and adjust this to reflect climatic changes derived from monthly average GCM results (Rosenzweig and Parry 1994). The problem for the study of extreme events is that, by the very nature of this approach, the mean is perturbed but the variability of the original observed time series is preserved.

An alternative approach is to use a statistical weather generator to derive long daily time series. Gregory et al (1993) give a critical appraisal of statistical models of precipitation generation. A common application of this technique is to generate daily rainfall series which can be input to crop-climate models, in order to study the effects of climate change on agriculture (for example Rackso et al 1991). However, the technique could also be used to examine the effect on the occurrence of extreme events of relevance to the insurance industry, such as episodes of heavy rainfall.

### Return periods

One problem for the insurance industry is that our knowledge of the present-day occurrence of extreme events is incomplete. For many parts of the world, meteorological records are too sparse and too short for statistical estimates of the return period of the extreme events to be calculated. This makes it difficult to interpret predictions of future changes in extreme event occurrence, since we are uncertain about the base upon which these changes may be superimposed. The recent occurrence of many events with lengthy 'return periods' shows the need for caution. Indeed, in some cases research has shown that the supposed return period, extrapolated from available scientific records, is contradicted by historical, 'unscientific' records (Anderson and Black 1993).

An example of an attempt to compile a long time series suitable for extreme event analysis is the United Kingdom Gale Index. Jenkinson and Collison (1977) provided guidelines for the calculation of this index extending back to 1881. Their approach has been used by a number of authors to calculate long time series of gale occurrence (Smith 1982, Hammond 1990, Hulme and Jones 1991). An example of this approach, for the number of winter gales over the region, is shown in Figure 6.4.

Data sets of this type are suitable for analysis using conventional statistical techniques, to identify the occurrence interval of extreme events. However, in order to apply these techniques it is necessary to assume that the time series is stable, ie that climate is not changing. Given that atmospheric concentrations of $CO_2$ have been increasing throughout the period over which the gale index of Figure 6.4 is constructed, and that global temperatures have increased by 0.5°C since the beginning of the century (Jones and Briffa 1992), it is not clear that this is a valid assumption.

### Coastal flooding and sea-level change

Global sea level can be expected to rise as a result of the greenhouse effect. Warrick and Oerlemans (1990), in their contribution to the 1990 IPCC report, arrived at a best estimate of 18.3cm for sea-level rise between 1985 and 2030. The major factor contributing to this increase is thermal expansion of sea water. Melting of mountain glaciers, and of the Greenland and Antarctic ice sheets, were shown to play a more minor role. In the 1992 IPCC report, the rate of change of sea level is given as between two and four centimetres per decade, due to thermal expansion alone (IPCC 1992, p17). This is broadly consistent with the IPCC 1990 figure.

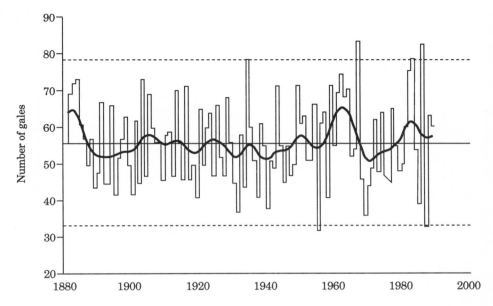

**Figure 6.4** *Number of gales per year over the UK region*

Note: gales defined by the Gale Index of Jenkinson and Collison (1977) calculated by P D Jones for the period 1881–1989 (see Hulme and Jones 1991, for a description of the method). The dotted lines are the two standard deviation limits calculated over the entire period. The smooth line is the 15-year Gaussian filter fitted through the series.
Source: Data presented here by kind permission of P D Jones

Sea level will not rise uniformly around the world, the change at a particular location may be quite different from the global change. Local and regional vertical land movements must be taken into account, and in some places will mask the effects of climate-related changes in ocean volume (Warrick and Oerlemans 1990). Changes in ocean dynamics and atmospheric pressure patterns are also important (Gregory 1993).

The risk of coastal flooding will become greater as a result of rising sea level. However, other factors will have an effect. For example, if there is an increase in the frequency of onshore winds at a particular location, then the risks will become greater regardless of sea-level rise. Coastal defences built following the 1953 flood made no allowance for sea-level rise. Much of Britain is now less than five metres above sea level, which is the common measure of the reach of an extreme storm surge.

### Tropical storms

Insurance and reinsurance companies in Britain have a major interest in covering risk overseas. Much of this is exposed to storm hazard in the Tropics. Haarsma et al (1993) found an increase in the number of tropical storms in the United Kingdom Meteorological Office (UKMO) GCM in a high-$CO_2$

world. However, there was no extension of the area affected. This result should be seen in the context of modelling work by Broccoli and Manabe (1990), who found an increase in the number of tropical storms as a result of global warming if cloud cover was prescribed, but a decrease if the cloud was generated within the model. It is now clear that tropical events are linked in a complex way, for example El Niño southern oscillation (ENSO) events appear to be associated with changes in the frequency, severity and track of Atlantic hurricanes (Glantz et al 1991). Whether or not these associations are well modelled by GCMs has not yet been thoroughly investigated.

### Mid- to high-latitude storms

No generalisations are possible about the effects of global warming on storm tracks in mid- to high latitudes, because studies which have been performed use different measures of storminess and address different regions (Gates et al 1992). These authors report that a significant reduction in the number of cyclonic events was found in the perturbed simulation of the Canadian Climate Centre GCM between 30°N and the North Pole in winter, but that this was associated with a significant increase in the number of strong cyclones. The high-resolution UKMO GCM $2xCO_2$ experiment indicates a north-westerly shift in storm tracks over the North Atlantic in winter (Hall et al 1994). Mullen and Renwick (1990) found an increase in storms over Australia and New Zealand in a high-$CO_2$ world.

Because the output from GCM is gridded, the effect of global warming on the United Kingdom Gale Index can be investigated using GCM simulations of mean sea-level pressure. An investigation based on the UKMO GCM indicated an increase in the frequency of gale days of around one-third (P R Rowntree, personal communication).

### Extreme rainfall events

Experiments with GCMs indicate a tendency for increased convective activity in a high-$CO_2$ world (Hansen et al 1989, Noda and Tokioka 1989). This implies an increase in the number of more intense local rain storms, and hence in runoff, at the expense of the gentler but more persistent rainfall events associated with larger-scale disturbances (Mitchell et al 1990). Supporting evidence for this is provided by Gordon et al (1992). In a model experiment with the Commonwealth Scientific and Industrial Research Organization (CSIRO) GCM, they found a general increase in the frequency of high-rainfall events and, in mid latitudes, a decrease in the number of rain days in the perturbed simulation. In two regional studies of Australia, Gordon et al (1992) and Whetton et al (1993) also found significantly increased daily rainfall intensities under $2xCO_2$ conditions.

### Drought

It is recognised that, as a result of greenhouse gas-induced warming, increases in potential evapotranspiration due to higher temperatures could increase drought potential even in regions where total rainfall increases

(Whetton et al 1993). Changes in drought potential can be estimated from GCM projections of future soil moisture conditions (see, for example, Manabe and Wetherald 1987). However, little confidence can be placed in the results, principally because surface hydrological processes are inadequately modelled in GCMs. A more satisfactory approach is to use a separate soil-water balance model initialised with GCM results of greater reliability, such as precipitation and temperature.

Whetton et al (1993) used this approach to examine the incidence of drought in Australia. They found the greatest changes in drought potential in the $2xCO_2$ simulation to be in the south of the country, with Mediterranean-type climates most at risk. Rind et al (1990) derived a drought index based on GCM output, and found increasing drought for the United States over the next century, but with effects detectable as early as the 1990s. Their results suggest that severe drought (with a 5 per cent frequency today) will occur about 50 per cent of the time by the 2050s. In the Mediterranean Sea region, decreases in moisture availability may be widespread (Palutikof et al 1994).

### Subsidence

A major cause of building subsidence is through the shrinkage of clay rich soils when soil moisture is lost. Hence, it is likely that the frequency and extent of subsidence will escalate in a warmer climate. The following analysis is based on a study currently underway at the Environmental Change Unit at the University of Oxford to identify regions in Europe potentially susceptible to drought-induced soil shrinkage and to assess the potential for subsidence being realised under global warming.

Subsidence potential will be realised only under certain conditions, namely through heating and drying which leads to soil moisture loss and soil shrinkage. The magnitude of shrinkage is a function of both the type of clay present and the intensity of drying conditions (Doornkamp 1993). Most residential buildings have a foundation depth of approximately one to three metres. Construction necessitates the removal of a certain amount of topsoil, generally up to a maximum of one metre. Hence, the soil profile depth which bears the greatest impact on building stability is the first four metres. The proportional clay content of the first four metres of soil within one degree grid cells across Europe was calculated. This was classified into areas with a high, moderate and low potential subsidence risk, based on thresholds employed by the US Department of Agriculture and the Soil Survey and Land Research Centre of England and Wales. Subsidence potential will be realised only under drying conditions. An index of drought was developed which balanced atmospheric moisture supply through precipitation with atmospheric moisture demand through evaporation. The subsidence risk from soil type was combined with the risk from drought and the present situation is depicted in Figure 6.5. Current regions with a high subsidence risk include south-west Spain and parts of eastern Europe, whilst south-east Spain, central France, eastern England and large areas of eastern Europe show a moderate risk.

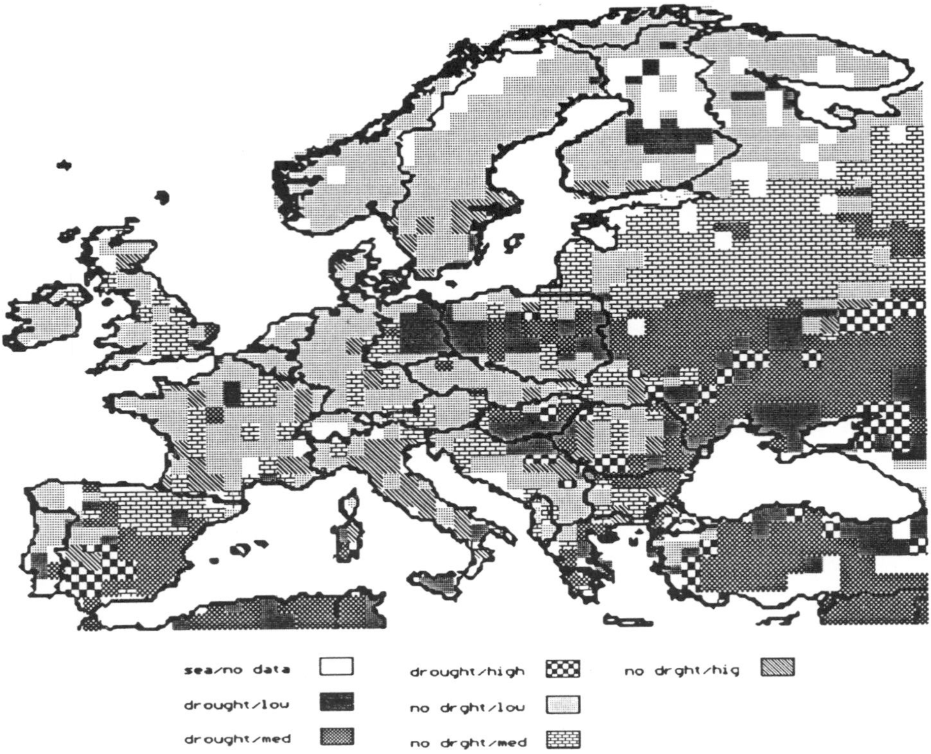
sea/no data
drought/lou
drought/med
drought/high
no drght/lou
no drght/med
no drght/hig

***Figure 6.5*** *Index of subsidence risk due to presence of clay-rich soils and drought conditions for the baseline (1951–80) climate*

Projections of how climate may change with global warming are provided by general circulation models. The output from two such models following an equivalent doubling of carbon dioxide in the atmosphere have been utilised: the Goddard Institute for Space Studies (GISS) model (Hansen et al 1984) and the Geophysical Fluid Dynamics Laboratory's (GFDL) model (Wetherald and Manabe 1986). As noted above, the direct output is not completely satisfactory, but the initial findings illustrate the issues which may arise. The risk of clay shrinkage-induced subsidence under these climate projections are shown in Figures 6.6 and 6.7. Under the GFDL projection the extent of land at risk from subsidence greatly increases. A high risk is indicated in south-west Spain, southern Scandinavia, northern Italy and isolated patches in south-east Europe. Much of eastern Europe and central Spain display a moderate risk, while northern France, southern Germany, Poland, Czechoslovakia and Romania are at low risk. The GISS projection indicates little change or decreased risk in eastern Europe. However, soils in Spain remain in the high-risk category, while France and south-east England display a moderate rather than low risk of subsidence.

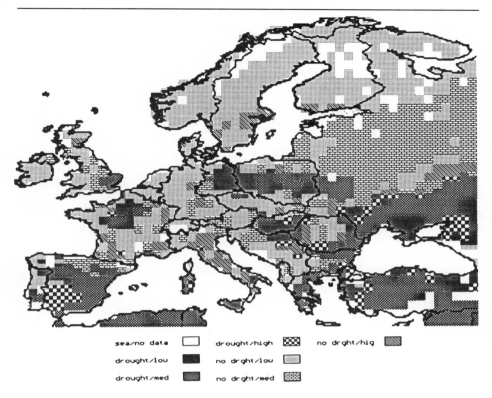

The legend includes: sea/no data, drought/high, no drght/hig, drought/lou, no drght/lou, drought/med, no drght/med

**Figure 6.6** *Subsidence risk from clay-rich soils and drought for the GISS $2xCO_2$ scenario of climate change*

To summarise, the extent to which clay-rich soils realise their shrinkage potential, and therefore cause damage to buildings, may increase with global warming. This may have a profound impact on the insurance industry. This approach cannot indicate exact locations and intensities of risk, due to paucity of data over such a large region. It can, however, be used to identify possible sensitive regions where more detailed small-scale assessments should be undertaken before the insurance industry decides on an appropriate response strategy.

### Freeze

Freeze events seem likely to diminish, particularly because minimum night-time temperatures have risen quite quickly, but this could be offset by two factors. First, increasing unfamiliarity may lead to a general relaxation of precautions. Secondly, there is some evidence, that the 'tail' of the frequency distribution is not Gaussian but more extended (Tol 1993).

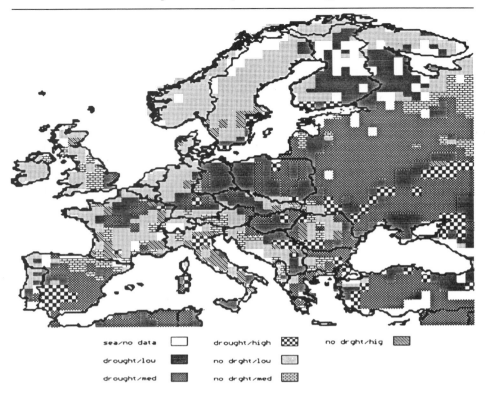

sea/no data ☐   drought/high ▨   no drght/hig ▨

drought/low ■   no drght/low ☐

drought/med ▨   no drght/med ▨

**Figure 6.7** *Subsidence risk from clay-rich soils and drought for the GFDL 2xCO₂ scenario of climate change*

## The Market

To a large extent the future vulnerability of the insurance industry will depend upon development unrelated to weather. The population of Britain will continue to grow slowly. The labour force will be static, or even shrink, as more attention goes to education and training. Family units will continue to become smaller in size as people live longer, and women become career-minded. The recent pattern of population growth will continue in southern counties with continued emphasis on growth in professional and business services. The new light industries do not need to be located near coal fields or ports, but rather near road links (Britain currently sends about seven times more freight by road than rail), and sources of skilled labour and housing. The single European Market and opening of the Channel Tunnel will intensify the advantage of a south-east location. Information technology will revolutionise the way we live and work, and transportation will alter to reflect this and concerns about pollution. In the less developed world, cities and industries will grow, creating large concentrations of risk, often in coastal regions and on flood plains.

A recent study by McKinsey foresees fewer independent insurers, more integration with other institutions/conglomerates, more direct marketing and more specialisation (Muth 1993). 'Services' competition in the European Union will be important in leading to greater uniformity in the insurance of natural hazards in Europe, in particular flood. The growth and success of the 'direct writers' of personal insurances could have implications for household insurance. The trend to telephone selling based on price could mitigate against more sophisticated underwriting and risk selection. The insurance press also predicts a move into direct selling of commercial packages, increasing the pressure for simplification of 'the product'. From the foregoing review of 'other factors' there is nothing which stands out as being capable of offsetting the potential increases in loss due to severe weather events. Indeed, business interruption exposures will probably worsen.

## Example of Loss Potential

It is useful at this juncture to illustrate the situation with some hypothetical calculations, to show how the size of a catastrophe compares with the financial strength of an insurer.

Suppose a large insurer covers a portfolio of domestic buildings and contents valued at £100,000 million (roughly one million homes), at an average rate of 0.3 per cent, giving an annual total premium at £300 million. In the rating, allowance is made for a catastrophe every ten years of £100 million, or £10 million per year. By law the insurer must hold free reserves equal to 17 per cent of the premium, but in practice 40 per cent is the working level, equivalent to £120 million. Clearly therefore, the fund can cope with the *average* catastrophe cost of £10 million per year, but it would be virtually wiped out in the year of the disaster. In 1987, the typical excess of loss reinsurance protection was equivalent to 30 per cent of the premium at risk, so in this example, £90 million of the risk was transferred. For this the insurer would pay a reinsurance premium somewhat higher than the annualised catastrophe cost, say £12 million.

Clearly if catastrophes become more frequent, the reinsurer suffers most. However, if catastrophes become larger, the insurer suffers. In fact by 1993, the insurer would have raised his protection to £200 million, but with a deductible of £30 million. At the same time, the reinsurer would have increased his charge to perhaps £75 million.

# Adaptation to Climate Change

Traditionally insurers have relied on four methods to cope with profit problems – limit the risk, control the claims, transfer the risk, or price the risk higher. The great danger is that funds will become less freely available, leading to the unavailability of insurance. This in turn will have consequences for other sectors, particularly banking, as assets may be unrepaired, or loans become non-performing. The consumer may also have to rely upon public relief following disasters, which is often haphazard and slow. Therefore a more radical set of solutions has to be initiated, involving dialogue with government and other parties, to improve the knowledge base.

## Limit the Risk

First consider the possibility of withdrawal. In high-risk areas overseas, this has already happened following catastrophic weather incidents. It is a natural course for insurers, who have a variety of markets where they can use their capital, perhaps more safely, and can be carried out quite quickly, since insurance contracts generally last for only 12 months. However insurers are not the only group affected. Financiers, banks and building societies, the occupiers (including insurance employees themselves), the construction industry, the designers, planners and architects, and local and national government (both nationally and internationally) would all be thrown into disarray. This means that if insurers collectively withdraw cover entirely for some peril, the authorities would have to react.

What is more likely in Britain is that all insurers might withdraw from some hazardous areas, or that some combinations of rating factors might become difficult to insure.

Alternatively insurers can limit the exposure whilst maintaining cover, the obvious one being to impose larger deductibles. (Within Britain the levels of deductible have traditionally been comparatively low.) There are various ways of doing this: imposing a larger monetary amount; using a deductible as a percentage of risk; or using a franchised deductible.

The use of first loss cover should be also considered as a way of limiting exposure to weather-related losses. This could be associated with differing sums insured at the same location based upon the same value at risk for differing perils. For example, a location prone to flooding might have an agreed value at risk of say £10 million but a first loss sum insured for flood perils of only £1 million. Traditionally first loss cover has been little encouraged within the British market, although is quite common overseas. The advantage is that it sets the limit of exposure to an identifiable and an acceptable figure as far as the insurer is concerned and encourages the occupier to ensure as far as practicable that his risk is minimised.

In conclusion, provided reinsurance capacity is available, the insurance market in Britain should be able to provide cover for the vast majority of risks, by using informal schemes and innovative underwriting to supplement standard procedures. Flood is the only hazard which is currently reinsured, but might encounter capacity problems. The key areas are East Anglia and the Thames estuary, where insurers should urgently examine their exposure on large industrial/commercial sites.

## Physical Risk Management and Loss Control

Risk management is primarily the function of avoiding damage by preparing for the event in advance. Loss control reduces the costs of the damage after the event by effective recovery. To be effective it is necessary to involve the potential loser by ensuring that a portion of any loss will fall upon the property user/owner, through co-insurance or a deductible.

Generally before land development is allowed permissions have to be obtained. Insurers can insist upon greater protective requirements for development within perceived high-risk areas, such as flood plains.

Within the construction sector losses can be controlled by identifying building standards required and adhering to them. Local authority departments should be heavily involved in monitoring the standards required together with the Building Research Establishment. Insurers are becoming involved through the Loss Prevention Council in Britain, because losses have increased so much, and often incorrect construction is to blame. Indeed, one of the great future issues will be how to 'retrofit' substandard buildings.

Local authorities are required to provide a capability to react to weather-related natural disasters but it is not usual to find adequate or similar considerations given by commercial organisations.

## Transfer the Risk

Reinsurance helps to spread the risk of a single catastrophe more widely but the capacity is not inexhaustible. The 1980s were a difficult period for property reinsurers – primarily the result of weather-related incidents – and the market capacity, whilst now recovering, was reduced substantially. In 1987, the reinsurance market supplied £1700 million capacity for British catastrophes. By 1990, this had risen to £3500 million, but fell to £2500 million in 1993, This figure is sufficient to cope with British storms, but floods could wipe it out.

The fundamental issue is that catastrophe insurance is long term, not suitable for accounting on an annual basis. A transfer of funds *across years* is required. Catastrophe or equalisation reserve funds are accumulated over a number of years, reducing the necessity to rely upon reinsurance arrangements, or shareholders' funds. Many countries exempt such funds from taxation and the British Government is now looking at this. The need for equalisation reserves is directly related to the increasing volatility of non-life insurers' claims experience worldwide. It is widely accepted that annual accounting is inappropriate for much non-life insurance business. Equalisation reserves would help to spread the impact of abnormally bad loss experience over a longer period of time.

A related issue is the funding of physical defences. At first sight it might seems that this 'insurance' should be charged to insurers, or policyholders, to recognise the risk reduction. However, this overlooks the fact that much of the benefit accrues to non-property owners, and also that many property owners do not, or would not, purchase insurance. On reflection this seems a burden suited for the taxation system, but insurers should reflect the quality of protections in their rates, so that local property owners do benefit.

## Price

Insurers' initial attitude might be merely to raise the premiums to increase the fund from which to meet potential losses. However, the price is usually derived from past losses. This method is flawed if the trend of increasing weather-related incidents continues. Recent 'return periods' of weather extremes are now substantially lower than for previous periods, with a consequent error in premiums being charged. To develop an accurate rating system more information is required on any changes in the pattern and frequency of storms and floods.

## Improve the Knowledge Base

There is a serious lack of knowledge internationally on weather patterns; the effect of climate change on these patterns; the effect of these changes on the potential for property loss and associated consequential costs; the value and specific locations and types of property at risk; and, lastly, of the actual losses sustained. As an example, the east coast of the USA had several decades almost free from hurricanes, lulling insurers into a false sense of security. Flooding from the sea is a potential area of disaster and the Association of British Insurers has now commissioned research to establish those areas of future high risk.

Research into changes in extreme weather is costly, and is often not generally available to the public domain. As a result, there is limited opportunity for insurers to act upon those areas considered necessary. From a practical viewpoint, the findings are not on a common database, and so are difficult to integrate. Furthermore the basic climate data is increasingly unavailable unless purchased.

Information on property and property losses is kept by insurers and other agencies but is confidential and often not retained for long. Providing access to such data, possibly through the Association of British Insurers, could have substantial benefits without necessarily affecting the confidentiality of information.

# Recommendations

## Insurers

• The insurance industry should be proactive in its approach to the problem of weather patterns and property insurance. This requires the different parties and levels of organisations to work together, whilst tackling the issues that properly concern them.

- Insurers and reinsurers should in principle provide cover against natural hazards, so far as compatible with commercial survival. To meet this imperative, they should explore through their trade bodies measures necessary to provide the necessary capacity at affordable premiums. This will involve a range of initiatives on risk management, information collection and analysis, and funding.
- Individual insurers should review their product covers and rating to ensure that there is an equitable sharing of the risk of weather damage. This could involve the use of first loss policies, larger deductibles, co-insurance, indemnity-only wordings, maintenance warranties and long-term contracts. Cover for high-risk items, and business interruption must be considered carefully.
- All insurance-related organisations should review their business strategies including investment to see that they take account of global warming and, wherever practical, that they help to mitigate it. This will involve committing resources to in-house projects, and also collaborative research initiatives.

Specific issues that need attention are:

- exposure to flood on the east coast of England and the Thames estuary, particularly on large commercial/industrial property;
- too-rigid acceptance procedures by insurers. Most 'heavy' risks can be underwritten;
- early attention should be given to archiving data on exposure and claims for future research.

## Other Financial Services

- Banks and other institutions concerned with credit and raising capital should take steps to learn about climate change.
- Climatic hazard should be treated as a factor which could affect the variability or profitability of core activities. Useful parallels may be drawn with the issue of lender liability arising from environmental impairment, where banks now examine carefully the risks which may derive from their clients' activities.
- Brokers and asset managers must recognise not only the direct impacts of climate change on economic sectors, but also that such important industries as tourism or energy may be indirectly affected by, say, the adaptive measures of insurers, or through goverment policy.

## The Authorities (Central and Local Government)

- Central and local government must provide leadership in the risk management of natural hazards, particularly flood. This entails research into the hazards themselves, and then taking the appropriate, preventive measures. Where appropriate, existing agencies must be prompted into action, and new interdisciplinary initiatives established, as recommended by the IPCC for Coastal Zone Management.
- Disaster plans must be made more open, and communicated more frequently.
- Central government must enact appropriate taxation rules to encourage insurers and reinsurers to accommodate catastrophe reserves.

Specific issues that need attention are:

- the difficulty of retro-fitting substandard buildings to satisfactory levels of solidity;
- climate data should be made available cheaply or even freely – they are a national resource, vital for risk management;
- research on past extremes is just as important as establishing future climatic trends.

# 7

# Greenhouse Policies and the Costs of Mitigation

## Introduction

The issue of potential climatic change is a global phenomenon, multifaceted, caused by a lot of different activities, affecting people in different places and in different ways. The set of possible policy measures to tackle global warming is similarly vast. This chapter is concerned with greenhouse mitigation strategies. However, to do justice to the global character of the problem, the chapter starts by drawing a general, global picture, which is eventually narrowed down to the issue of global warming mitigation in Britain, and the rest of the European Union.

In analysing the scope of greenhouse mitigation policies, we distinguish between two types of policy options, global warming prevention (or greenhouse-gas abatement) on the one hand, and adaptation (or climate change protection) on the other. Greenhouse mitigation should be designed such that the overall harm to society is kept as low as possible. Economists would phrase this as advocating the use of the economic efficiency criterion for both sets of policies. Basically, efficiency requires that further action is undertaken as long as the incremental costs of doing so are smaller than the additional benefits in the form of mitigated damage. There is a strong linkage between prevention and adaptation policies, and in an ideal world the two sets of policies would therefore have to be implemented simultaneously.

The chapter is divided into two parts. The first part contains some general thoughts about greenhouse mitigation, the idea of economic efficiency and the relative importance of prevention and adaptation policies, drawing on examples from several sources and for several countries. The latter part of the chapter contains numerical examples of these general principles, using the PAGE model (Hope et al 1993), which provides an integrated framework for such analysis, and shows how far ideas of economic efficiency can be taken with knowledge in its present state.

# Greenhouse Prevention vs Adaptation

In the introduction we have argued that policy makers loosely have two sets of options to moderate the impacts of greenhouse warming.* They can either limit the amount of greenhouse gases emitted – the well-known abatement option, leading to a lower degree of warming – or they can ease the impacts of a given change through appropriate protection measures. The former option we call climate change *prevention*, the latter *adaptation*. Adaptation activities may include such examples as the development of heat-resistant crops, a change in agricultural and forest management, the building of dykes and sea walls, the construction of water storage and irrigation systems and the adaptation of houses. Schelling (1992) has even argued that for developing countries the best adaptation strategy may simply be economic development. Both sets of options, prevention and adaptation, have to be taken into account when drafting the greenhouse policy response.

Analytically, the optimal combination of prevention and adaptation can be found by minimising the total costs of climate change, consisting of the costs of emissions abatement $PC$,** the costs of adaptation $AC$ and the costs of greenhouse damage D:

$$min_{p,a} \quad AC(a) + PC(p) + D(T,a)$$

subject to $T = f(p)$

where $p$ denotes the level of prevention (emissions abatement), and $a$ the degree of adaptation. Climate change is symbolised by the variable $T$ (for temperature change), and depends negatively on the amount of greenhouse prevention $p$: The higher the abatement effort, the lower the temperature increase. Greenhouse damage $D$ depends positively on the temperature level, $T$, and negatively on the amount of adaptation, $a$; $AC$ and $PC$ both depend positively on their arguments.

The optimal conditions for this simultaneous optimisation problem require that the marginal costs of each policy measure be equal to the benefits of prevented or mitigated warming, respectively.*** This is the standard cost-benefit result. *Further preventive steps are justified as long as the incremental costs of doing so are smaller than the additional benefits from warming avoided. Similarly, further adaptation is warranted as long as the additional costs are lower than the additional benefits.* Graphically, we seek the intersection of the marginal cost curve with the respective marginal benefits curve (Figure 7.1). Both decisions are thus made according to the same criterion of economic efficiency, although extensions to it may be necessary under some circumstances, as will be argued below. It is important to note that the optimal value for each option depends on the value chosen for the

---

* The following exposition is drawing on Fankhauser 1994b
** Climate change prevention policies may also include geo-engineering. This option has gained little attention in the literature so far and we abstract from it here.
*** Formally, $PC' = -D_T f'$, and $AC' = -D_a$

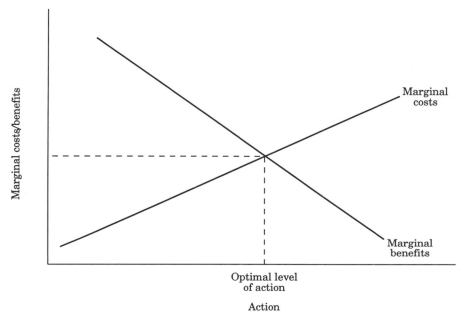

**Figure 7.1** *The optimal level of greenhouse mitigation action*

other. If significant preventive measures are taken, little action may be needed with respect to adaptation. Conversely, if the consequences of global warming can easily and cheaply be adapted to, there may be little need for preventive carbon abatement. The two sets of policy measures should thus be carefully coordinated, and would ideally be determined simultaneously.

## Greenhouse Adaptation Measures

It seems evident that society will not just sit still and suffer in the face of climate change. People will react and adjust to the new conditions. Farmers will try to increase irrigation and utilise different crops, house owners will replace heaters with air conditioning devices, some coastlines may be protected by sea walls, and so on. Much of the adaptive action will probably happen on an individual level, for example the gradual adjustment of people's lifestyles. In addition, adaptive action will also be necessary from the public sector, for example in the case of coastal protection. This will leave policy makers with the difficult task of deciding on the optimal level of protection, most often without knowing the exact amount of climate change to be expected. In the previous section we have argued that, as a general rule, adaptation should take place as long as the benefits from avoided damage exceed the incremental costs of additional action.

The question of adaptation is not only a challenge to policy makers, but also to damage modellers, who have to predict the extent of protective measures likely to be taken, on both individual and collective levels, before they can assess the net greenhouse damage which will occur as a result. In a world with adaptation, the costs of global warming will consist of two parts: the costs of the adaptive measures, plus the costs of the remaining, unmitigated damage. Thus, in the case of sea-level rise, for example, costs will occur in the form of increased sea defence expenditures, and as a loss of coastal land in unprotected areas.

Greenhouse adaptation can potentially be a very powerful option. Yet, with the notable exception of sea-level rise, so far its importance has often been neglected in the literature. In the remainder of the section we will give two illustrations of how important adaptation may be in minimising the costs of global warming.

## Example I: Agriculture

A good example for the difficulties of predicting adaptation on an individual level is agriculture. It is likely that through an appropriate change in farm management, it will be possible to cancel out the most adverse effects of global warming on agriculture and food supply. Yet many, at least earlier, agricultural damage assessments have neglected this point and may thus have overestimated true damage. The assumption of zero adaptation is often termed the 'dumb farmer' hypothesis – farmers are assumed to continue planting the same crops, even though climatic conditions have altered. Recognising this simplification, recent work has tried to incorporate managerial responses into agricultural models (Rosenzweig and Parry 1994, Easterling et al 1993 and Mendelsohn et al 1992). The quantitative difference which can occur from the inclusion of adaptation is probably best exemplified in the study by Easterling et al (1993), which calculates agricultural damage both with and without adaptation.

As part of the MINK project (see Crosson and Rosenberg 1993), Easterling et al have estimated the impact of climate change on the agricultural sector in the four American states of Missouri, Iowa, Nebraska and Kansas, using the hot and dry climate of the 1930s as an analogue. A selection of their results is reproduced in Table 7.1.

Adaptation strategies were by and large limited to low-cost, already available responses such as increased irrigation, earlier planting and the use of longer-season varieties. As a result of such measures it may be possible to reduce agricultural damage to the region by as much as 60 per cent, from $1329 million to $532 million (see Table 7.1). The figures are based on 1984–87 production and include $CO_2$ fertilisation.* Without $CO_2$ enrichment the effect of adaptation would only be about 30 per cent, a figure which would again mount to about 60 per cent for the economy of the year 2030. These fig-

---

*Many crop plants such as wheat respond to higher levels of $CO_2$ in the atmosphere by increasing their rate of photosynthesis (Parry 1990).

***Table 7.1*** *Climate-induced changes in MINK crop production*

| | No adjustment | | Including adjustment | |
|---|---|---|---|---|
| | m$ (1982) | % | m$ (1982) | % |
| Corn | −1035 | −13.4 | −1236 | −16.0 |
| Wheat | 150 | 8.2 | 361 | 19.7 |
| Sorghum | −118 | −9.4 | 178 | 14.1 |
| Soybeans | −438 | −12.8 | −48 | −1.4 |
| Hay | 112 | 7.0 | 435 | 27.3 |
| *Total* | *−1329* | *−8.4* | *−532* | *−3.3* |

1984–87 averages, including $CO_2$ enrichment.
Source: Easterling et al 1993

ures are not, of course, transferable to the case of British agriculture, where climate as well as the agricultural system are very different. Yet, they give a clear indication of how important agricultural adaptation may be.

## Example II: Climate Amenity and Heat Stress

A study carried out for the US Environmental Protection Agency suggests that as a result of global warming US electricity demand may rise by about 1.4 per cent for a 1.2°C temperature rise and by 5.2 per cent for 3.7°C, due to an increased demand in air conditioning (Smith and Tirpak 1989). Increased air conditioning is a typical example of a climate change-induced adaptive measure, taken on an individual level. Additional income, which would otherwise have been used for consumption, is spent on reducing (inside) air temperature to a more pleasant level. Assuming an electricity price of 7.5 cents/kwh, avertive expenditures would amount to $3–11 billion for the US. Arguably, excessive heat may be less of a problem in a more northern country like Britain. It may well be that global warming will lead to an overall reduction in energy demand for this country, due to reduced heating expenses – the reversed form of defensive action against climate disamenity (see Chapter 5 in this volume).

Adaptation of this sort would not only help to improve the well-being associated with a certain climate, it may also have an important impact on the number of casualties caused by extreme temperature events. This can be illustrated by another US study commissioned by the Environmental Protection Agency, which attempts to estimate the impact of global warming on mortality and heat stress casualties for 15 US cities (Kalkstein 1989). The study produces two sets of estimates. The first set is achieved by feeding global warming data into a statistical model regressing mortality on climate variables. This approach allows for only limited acclimatisation, and estimates are correspondingly high, about 300 summer casualties per million inhabitants. In a second set of estimates, Kalkstein uses analogues as a better means of capturing morbidity impacts under full acclimatisation. With acclimatisation the increase in summer mortality is only 49 deaths per million, one-sixth of the initial number.

Because of the different methods used, the two pairs of estimates are not directly comparable, and are partly contradicting. Yet, even if the Kalkstein figures may be debatable in many respects, they clearly underline the importance of acclimatisation, showing that cities already accustomed to a warmer climate are far less affected by a further warming than cities with a moderate climate.* Much of this process will probably happen automatically, even though acclimatisation includes much more than just biological and behavioural adjustment. Acclimatisation may for example also require a change in the physical structure of a city (such as by using a different building style, and more reflecting materials), a fact which town planners and architects will have to be aware of.

## Global Warming Prevention

Britain accounts for about 3 per cent of total greenhouse gas emissions (World Resources Institute 1992). While this is a higher share than that of most other countries in the world, it is still small. Britain therefore, does not have the power markedly to influence global greenhouse gas emissions on its own. Like most other OECD nations, Britain has committed itself to a reduction in its emissions to 1990 levels by the year 2000. Whether this target is sensible and sufficient has therefore to be judged in an international context, where this country's commitment is only one aspect of a worldwide effort to combat global warming.

In its 1990 assessment the IPCC stated that a 60 per cent reduction in the current level of greenhouse gas emissions would be necessary in order to stabilise atmospheric concentrations (IPCC 1990). This, and many similar targets, are in stark contrast to what policy makers are currently willing to do. The Rio scenario of emissions returning to their 1990 levels by 2000 in developed countries, for example, translates into an emissions cut of under 7 per cent compared to business as usual in Britain (Department of the Environment 1992). Stringent targets are also in contrast to the recommendations of most cost-benefit assessments (CBA) of climate change, that is to the numerical results from the approach presented in the section above on prevention vs adaptation. Two benchmark cost figures are available which underlie most CBA assessments:

- Damage costs: the costs associated with an atmospheric $CO_2$ concentration doubling has been calculated to be in the order of about 1–2 per cent of GNP.

---

*This to an extent that some of Kalkstein's estimates actually show a *decrease* in summer mortality, the negative from warming being more than offset by the better acclimitisation in the chosen analogue.

- Abatement costs: a 50 per cent cut from 'business as usual' emissions by 2020–50 may reduce GNP by about 1–3 per cent of GNP (Cline 1994, Fankhauser 1994a).

One prominent cost-benefit model, DICE (Dynamic Integrated Climate Economy model; Nordhaus 1993a,b), calculates that, on the basis of the above benchmarks, optimal carbon emissions would only be about 10 per cent below business-as-usual levels in the year 2000, and 15 per cent in 2100. However, this low abatement conclusion does not generally hold. Cline (1992), for example, has found much higher abatement levels to be optimal, after having altered some of Nordhaus' more crucial assumptions, in particular about the discount rate. Nevertheless, there does seem to be a tendency for CBA results not to give support to calls for immediate and strong action.

# The PAGE Model

When things are as uncertain as this, there is a need to pay serious attention to uncertainty, and the effect it can have on policy recommendations. One model in which uncertainty plays a central role is the PAGE model for Policy Analysis of the Greenhouse Effect, developed by Hope et al (1993). The general form of the PAGE model is shown in Figure 7.2. It was designed to provide insights for policy makers even where great uncertainty exists. It contains a highly simplified climate model which calculates the global mean temperature resulting from the emissions of greenhouse gases, a routine to calculate the ensuing economic impacts, and modules which calculate the costs of policies to prevent the build-up of greenhouse gases, and to adapt to any climate change that still occurs (a full description of PAGE is given in Hope et al 1993).

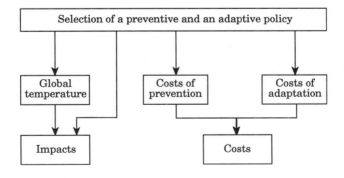

***Figure 7.2*** *The form of the PAGE model*

PAGE contains equations that cover the following:

- **The European Union and the whole world**. Although PAGE was developed for European Community policy makers, the greenhouse effect is a global problem. European Union emissions of carbon dioxide are only 13 per cent of the world total. PAGE takes account of the gains to the European Union of emission controls in the rest of the world. The global mixing of greenhouse gases also means that no region can justify large cutbacks in greenhouse gas emissions by reference to the benefits in that region alone. PAGE therefore takes into account the effect on the rest of the world of European Union emission controls. Calculations are therefore made for four world regions (currently implemented as the European Union, rest of the OECD, the former Soviet Union and Eastern Europe, and rest of the world).
- **The whole of the next century**. Greenhouse gases emitted today are likely to continue having a warming effect for decades. The discounted costs of emission controls are much higher if they are made in 2000 rather than 2050. The analysis in PAGE covers the period 1990 to 2100.
- **All major greenhouse gases**. Global temperature change is calculated not just from the emissions of carbon dioxide, but also from the emissions of methane, CFCs and HCFCs.
- **The impacts of global warming**. Changes in global mean temperature are compared to the maximum changes that can be tolerated, and weighting factors are applied to calculate the impacts brought about by global warming in up to ten sectors of the economy. In the application reported in this chapter, seven sectors are used to represent economic impacts, and an eighth to capture non-economic environmental and social impacts.
- **The costs of emission controls**. Comparison with reductions in the impacts of global warming give an indication of the justification at regional and global levels for policies which would control the emissions of greenhouse gases.
- **The costs of adaptation**. Comparison with reductions in the impacts from global warming give an indication of the justification at regional and global levels for measures to adapt to a changed climate.
- **The effects of uncertainty**. The challenge for all greenhouse gas models is to say something useful for policy makers in a situation of profound uncertainty. The only way to meet that challenge was to incorporate uncertainty into PAGE from the start. More than 80 key input parameters are expressed as probability distributions, and all uncertainties are carried through the calculation so that their effect on any result can be found.

PAGE can therefore be used to judge the merits of policies to control the emissions of greenhouse gases, and policies to adapt to any climate change that does occur. It automatically incorporates the uncertainty that is the major obstacle to policy making, and allows the critical uncertainties to be found.

# Costs and Economic Benefits of Prevention

Two preventive policies are examined in this application with PAGE. There are clearly many other possible policies, but these two are chosen as reasonable representatives of the emissions that might result from unconcern and concern about global warming respectively:

1. A 'no-action' policy, with no special measures being taken to reduce or slow the growth in emissions of greenhouse gases in the European Union or any other world region. (Global emissions of carbon dioxide rise by about 200 per cent from their 1990 levels by 2100.)
2. An 'aggressive' policy, based on a global package of stringent controls, for instance including a carbon tax, a shift to low carbon fuels and improved energy efficiency.

The carbon dioxide emissions of the two policies in the four world regions are shown in Figure 7.3. With 'no-action', emissions rise in all four regions, but the greatest growth by far is seen in the developing countries of the 'rest of the world' region.

With an 'aggressive' policy, emissions still rise in the developing countries, but at a much slower rate, and absolute emission reductions are seen in other regions. In the world as a whole, carbon dioxide emissions still rise by about 60 per cent from their 1990 levels by 2100.

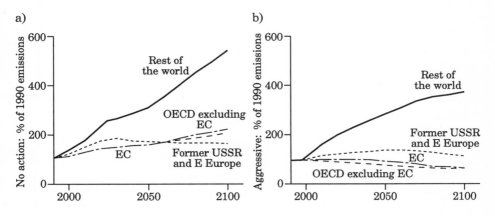

***Figure 7.3*** *$CO_2$ emissions under two preventive policies:*
*a) no action, b) aggressive policy*

The obvious comparison to make is between the costs of the control measures incorporated in the 'aggressive' prevention policy and the reduction in economic impacts that the 'aggressive' prevention policy might bring. Table 7.2 shows the result of this comparison for the world as a whole. At a 5 per cent discount rate, the mean results show the extra global costs of control, at $2.7 trillion, just outweighing the $2 trillion global benefits from the reduction in economic impacts. Only if the costs of control are towards the lower end of the range of estimates, or if a lower discount rate than 5 per cent per year is thought to be appropriate, would the direct economic benefits from the 'aggressive' preventive policy outweigh its costs.

**Table 7.2** *Global economic benefits and costs of aggressive prevention*

| 1995–2100 | Trillion dollars[a] | | |
|---|---|---|---|
| | Minimum | Mean | Maximum |
| Benefits | 0.5 | 2.0 | 3.4 |
| Costs | 0.8 | 2.7 | 5.7 |

[a] In European Currency Units in the original publication, converted to $US at the rate of 1 to 1.
Source: Hope et al 1993

In the European Union region and the rest of the OECD, based on the mean results and at a 5 per cent discount rate, the costs of the 'aggressive' preventive policy are justified by the reduction in direct economic impacts. However, as we commented above, it would not seem sensible to try to tackle global warming by prevention alone; however draconian the cutbacks in emissions, some warming and consequent economic impacts will occur, and so adaptation to that warming will also need to be considered.

## Costs and Economic Benefits of Adaptation

Adaptive policies include such measures as the building of sea walls, better management of water resources, land-use planning to prevent development in vulnerable areas and changes in the types of crops grown.

As with preventive policies, two adaptive policies are examined in this application:

1. A policy representing 'no-action' as far as adaptive measures are concerned. Impacts are accepted as and when they occur. This is the adaptive policy that was assumed in the calculations of the global economic benefit from the 'aggressive' preventive policy shown in Table 7.2.
2. An 'aggressive' package of adaptive measures, based primarily on mitigation of impacts due to water resource changes and sea-level rise. Work is assumed to start on the adaptive policy in the near future, and its effect is to make a global temperature rise of 2°C tolerable in all sectors by 2000. If the global temperature rise exceeds 2°C, land-use planning measures are assumed to reduce the economic impacts for each additional degree centigrade of temperature rise by up to 90 per cent by 2050, except for agriculture in the developing countries, where the pressure of population is assumed to make adaptive measures only 50 per cent effective at all levels of temperature rise.

As with the 'aggressive' preventive policy, the basic comparison is between the costs of 'aggressive' adaptation and the reduction in economic impacts that the 'aggressive' adaptive policy would bring. Table 7.3 shows this comparison. At a 5 per cent discount rate, the mean results show that the costs of adaptation, at about half a trillion dollars, are easily justified by the $17.5 trillion benefits from the reduction in economic impacts.

**Table 7.3** *Global economic benefits and costs of aggressive adaptation*

| 1995–2100 | Trillion dollars[a] | | |
|---|---|---|---|
| | Minimum | Mean | Maximum |
| Benefits | 5.5 | 17.5 | 27.0 |
| Costs | –[b] | 0.5 | 1.0 |

[a] In European Currency Units in the original publication, converted to $US at the rate of 1 to 1
[b] less than 1/4 trillion dollars
Source: Hope et al 1993

The remaining economic impacts to 2100, if 'aggressive' adaptation is introduced, have a mean value of only about $0.3 trillion worldwide at a 5 per cent discount rate. Therefore adaptation is very effective at reducing the worldwide economic impacts from global warming.

With such a strong excess of benefits over costs at the global level, it is no surprise that the 'aggressive' adaptive policy is economically worthwhile in every region. An additional advantage is that all of the benefit from its introduction is captured in the region that incurs the costs. Adaptation is notably different from prevention in this respect.

Despite all the uncertainties, the argument for introducing an aggressive adaptive policy is very strong. Plans should be made to start introducing sea defences, water resource management, and land-use planning measures in all regions. Since they will take several decades to have their full effect, their implementation should start as soon as possible.

Therefore it is against the background of the much smaller worldwide economic damage after 'aggressive' adaptation that the case for prevention has to be made. It is clear that if 'aggressive' prevention cannot be justified by the reduction in worldwide economic impacts with no adaptation, it certainly cannot be justified by pointing to a reduction in the much smaller economic impacts that remain after adaptation.

## The Case for a Combined Policy

Does this mean there is no scope for global warming prevention at national, regional or global levels? It does not. There are several lines of argument, expanding on the notion of economic efficiency, which are capable of justifying higher prevention levels. They include precautionary and equity considerations, as well as the existence of non-economic impacts and non-global warming benefits.

## Non-Economic Impacts

Relying solely upon adaptation runs the risk of potentially severe and irreversible impacts upon society of a quite different kind from the direct economic impacts that have been considered so far. The environmental and social consequences of global warming which do not enter directly into the calculation of economic impacts but which could nevertheless be significant include:

- inundation and permanent loss of coastal locations with particular social, natural or educational value;
- loss of biodiversity, natural habitats, nature reserves and areas of special scientific interest, for instance through the inability of ecosystems to migrate sufficiently rapidly in response to shifting climatic zones;
- a lower quality of life through environmental degradation and health effects, for instance from the interaction between climatic extremes and pollution, from the spread of disease with climatic and vegetation shifts, and from the degradation of water resources in less developed regions;
- loss of human life through coastal flooding, natural hazards, health effects and regional degradation of the socio-economic resource base;
- the societal, cultural and security implications of large-scale migration;
- local transitional pressures resulting from economic decay in some regions and sectors, and the problems of re-structuring to take advantage of new economic opportunities elsewhere.

These impacts cannot easily be estimated. While an ad hoc assessment of some non-market impacts is included in the 1–2 per cent damage range mentioned above, none of the PAGE results reported here have included them. However, with PAGE we can calculate how such environmental and social impacts would have to be valued in order that a particular combination of preventive and adaptive policies (namely 'aggressive' prevention combined with 'aggressive' adaptation) would be considered a worthwhile option, both for individual regions and for the world as a whole.

Table 7.4 shows the weight that needs to be placed upon environmental and social impacts, as a multiple of the modal weight on all economic impacts combined, for the mean value of a combined strategy of 'aggressive' prevention with 'aggressive' adaptation to be preferred to adaptation alone. In this calculation it is assumed that adaptive measures would be largely ineffective against environmental and social impacts. This may overstate the difficulty of dealing with these impacts since, for instance, land-use planning would prevent some of the loss of life that would otherwise occur with increased flooding in developing countries.

**Table 7.4** *Non-economic impacts required to justify a combined strategy, by region taking action*

| Region | Multiple of economic impact |
|---|---|
| European Union alone | 15 |
| Whole of OECD | 3 |
| Worldwide | 2 |

Source: Hope et al 1993

Because the effect of a preventive policy is to reduce the rise in global temperature, some of its benefits are received outside the region adopting the policy. The results in Table 7.4 show how important it would be for the European Union to persuade at least its main trading partners in the rest of the OECD to adopt the combined strategy as well.

Environmental and social values would have to be about 15 times the sum of all economic impacts if the European Union were to introduce the combined strategy alone, and expect to see a sufficient reduction in impacts just in its own member states. However, if the whole of the OECD were to introduce the combined strategy, the corresponding valuation of environmental and social impacts would need to be only about three times direct economic impacts. This does not fall much further if the whole world were to adopt a combined strategy; a valuation of environmental and social impacts of twice the sum of direct economic impacts would still be required for adoption of the combined strategy to be justified.

## Non-Global Warming Benefits

### Spillovers

The impacts of prevention measures will not be limited to global warming alone, but are likely to spill over to other sectors. It appears that most of these spillovers are positive in nature, and this may help to justify more action than would otherwise be the case. For example, $CO_2$ abatement may lead to an improvement in air quality through a parallel reduction in the emissions of classic air pollutants, such as $SO_2$. These effects are called the 'secondary benefits' of carbon abatement.

### Revenue recycling

If abatement is brought about by an environmental tax (for example a carbon tax), the resulting revenues can be used to lower other, distortionary taxes, such as those on labour. This will lower the welfare costs of governmental revenue raising – the so called 'double dividend' of carbon abatement. Some researchers have suggested that with appropriate revenue recycling, the costs of carbon abatement can be reduced enormously from the engineering-based values used in the PAGE calculation (Barker et al 1993).

## Uncertainty

Most CBA results are based on assessments of the most likely damage outcome, usually on the case of atmospheric $CO_2$ concentration doubling ($2xCO_2$). However, climate uncertainty is such that other, much worse scenarios cannot be excluded with certainty. Scientists (and economists) might have got it wrong. Surprises may occur, particularly in the long run. This is why the PAGE model works with probability distributions rather than single values, but even the PAGE results do not include the kind of catastrophic changes described in Leggett (1991). A risk-averse society may want to hedge against the possibility of unpleasant outcomes by undertaking precautionary abatement. Greenhouse prevention would then function as a sort of climate insurance (Manne and Richels 1991).

## Equity

### *Inter-generational equity*
The issue of global warming is a long-term problem, and damages stemming from the greenhouse effect would mainly affect as yet unborn generations of people. In the PAGE calculations reported here, costs and impacts are both discounted at 5 per cent per annum. Some would argue that this rate is inappropriately high for impacts that may occur a century or more into the future. Additional greenhouse gas abatement may thus be justified for ethical reasons, if it is considered morally wrong to expose future generations to the climate impacts caused by our current actions.

### *International equity*
Most CBA calculations ignore distributional considerations, and the PAGE results reported here are no exception. A million dollars of costs or benefits is given the same weight, whether it occurs in the rich countries of Europe, or the poor ones of Africa. There is an alternative view, forcefully expressed at occasions such as the Rio conference, that the rich countries are predominantly responsible for the global warming problem, and so it is only fair if they bear the main costs of preventing the problem worsening in the future (Agarwal and Narain 1991).

Although not all of these ideas have yet been put into operation fully, they all seem to justify additional greenhouse prevention measures in Britain and Europe. However, if this is so, we should be clear about why further prevention is warranted. The justification comes much more from ethical and precautionary considerations, than from the actual economic damage the world is most likely to face in the foreseeable future.

# References

## Chapter 1 Background to Possible Changes in the British Climate

CCIRG (Climatic Change Impacts Review Group) 1991 *The Potential Effects of Climate Change in the United Kingdom* UK DoE Report Publication, HMSO

Hadley Centre 1992 *The Hadley Centre Transient Climate Change Experiment* Hadley Centre, Bracknell, August

IPCC (Houghton, J T, Jenkins, G J, and Ephraums, J J (eds)) 1990 *Climate Change: The IPCC Scientific Assessment* Cambridge University Press

IPCC (Houghton, J T, Callander, B A, and Varney, S K (eds)) 1992 *Climate Change 1992: The Supplementary Report to the IPCC Scientific Assessment* Cambridge University Press

IPCC (1996 forthcoming) The Second Assessment Report

Viner, D and Hulme, M 1994 *The Climate Impacts LINK Project. Providing Climate Change Scenarios for Impact Assessments in the UK* Climatic Research Unit, University of East Anglia

Wigley, T M L and Raper, S C B, 1992 'Implications for climate and sea level of revised IPCC emissions scenarios' *Nature* 357 pp293–300

## Chapter 2 The Effects of Sea-level Rise

Arnell, N W, Jenkins, A and George, D G 1994 *The Implications of Climate Change for the National Rivers Authority* R & D Report 12 NRA, Bristol

Ball, J H, Clark, M J, Collins, M B, Gao, S, Ingham, A, and Ulph, A 1991 *The Economic Consequences of Sea Level Rise on the Central Southern Coast of England* GeoData Institute Report to MAFF, University of Southampton

Clark, J A and Primus, J A 1987 'Sea level changes resulting from future retreat of ice sheets: an effect of $CO_2$ warming of the climate' In, Tooley, M J and Shennan, I (eds) *Sea level Changes* Basil Blackwell, Oxford pp356–370

Clark, J A, Farrell, W E and Peltier, W R 1978 'Global changes in post-glacial sea level: a numerical calculation' *Quaternary Research* 9 pp265–287

Coker, A M, Thompson, P M, Smith, D I and Penning-Rowsell, E C 1989 'The impact of climate change on coastal zone management in Britain: a preliminary analysis' *The Publications of the Academy of Finland 9/89. Conference on Climate and Water 2* pp148–160

Davidson, N C, Laffoley, D d'A, Doody, J P, Way, L S, Gordon, J, Key, R, Drake, C M, Pienkowski, M W, Mitchell, R and Duff, K L 1991 *Nature Conservation and Estuaries in Great Britain* Nature Conservancy Council, Peterborough

den Elzen, M and Rotmans, J 1992 'The socio-economic impact of sea-level rise on the Netherlands: a study of possible scenarios' *Climatic Change* 20 pp169–195

Department of the Environment/Welsh Office 1992 *Planning Policy Guidance: Coastal Planning* PPG20 HMSO, London

Fankhauser, S 1994 'Protection versus retreat: the economic costs of sea-level rise' *Environment and Planning A* forthcoming

Gornitz, V 1993 'Mean sea-level changes in the recent past' In, Warrick, R A, Barrow, E M and Wigley, T M L (eds) *Climate and Sea-Level Change: observations projections and implications* Cambridge University Press pp25–44

Greensmith, J T and Tooley, M J (eds) 1982 'IGCP Project 61. Sea-level movements during the last deglacial hemicycle (about 15,000 years) Final Report of the UK Working Group' *Proceedings of the Geological Association* 93 pp1–128

Hageman, B P 1969 'Development of the western part of the Netherlands during the Holocene' *Geol. Mijn.* 48 (4) pp373–88

Hoffman, J S 1984 'Estimates of future sea-level rise' In, Barth, M C and Titus, J (eds) *Greenhouse Effect and Sea-Level Rise: a Challenge for this Generation* van Nostrand Reinhold, New York pp79–103

Holt, T 1991 *Storm Conditions over the North Sea: A Historical Perspective and Implications for the 21st Century* Report to NRA, Climatic Research Unit, University of East Anglia, Norwich

Hutchinson, J 1980 'The record of peat wastage in the East Anglian Fenlands at Holme Post, 1848–1978 AD' *Journal of Ecology* 68 pp229–249

IPCC (Houghton, J T, Callander, B A, and Varney, S K (eds)) 1992 *Climate Change 1992: The Supplementary Report to the IPCC Scientific Assessment* Cambridge University Press

IPCC (Houghton, J T, Jenkins, G J, and Ephraums, J J (eds)) 1990a *Climate Change: The IPCC Scientific Assessment* Cambridge University Press

IPCC 1990b *Strategies for Adaptation to Sea-Level Rise. Report of the Coastal Zone Management Subgroup* WMO and UNEP, Geneva

IPCC, CZMS 1992 *Global Climate Change and the Rising Challenge of the Sea* WMO and UNEP, Geneva

Lee, E M 1993 'The political ecology of coastal planning and management in England and Wales: policy responses to the implications of sea-level rise' *The Geographical Journal* 159 pp169–178

Milliman, J F, Broadus, J M and Gable, F 1989 'Environmental and economic implications of rising sea level and subsiding deltas: the Nile and Bengal examples' *Ambio* 18 pp340–345

Ministry of Agriculture, Fisheries and Food 1993a *Strategy for Flood and Coastal Defence* MAFF, London

Ministry of Agriculture, Fisheries and Food 1993b *Coastal Defence Works and the Environment: A Guide to Good Practice* MAFF, London

National Audit Office 1992 *Coastal Defences in England* HMSO, London

Proudman Oceanographic Laboratory (POL) 1993 Internal Report to MAFF, unpublished

Pye, K and French, P W 1993 'Targets for coastal habitat re-creation' *English Nature Science* 13, English Nature, Peterborough

Rossiter, J R 1962 'Long term variations in sea level' In, Hill, N M (ed) *The Sea* 1 pp590–610, Interscience Publishers, London

Shaw, J 1989 'Drumlins, subglacial meltwater floods, and ocean responses' *Geology* 17 pp853–6

Shennan, I 1989 'Holocene crustal movements in Great Britain' *Journal of Quaternary Science* 4 pp77–89

Shennan, I 1993 'Sea-level changes and the threat of coastal inundation' *Geographical Journal* 159 (2) pp148–156

Shennan, I 1987 'Holocene sea-level changes in the North Sea region' In, Tooley, M J and Shennan, I (eds) *Sea-Level Changes* Basil Blackwell, Oxford pp109–151

Shennan, I, Orford, J and Plater, A (eds) 1992 'IGCP Project 274: Quaternary coastal evolution: case studies, models and regional patterns. Final report of the UK Working Group' *Proceedings of the Geological Association* 103(3) pp163–272

Streif, H 1989 'Barrier islands, tidal flats and coastal marshes resulting from a relative rise of sea level in East Frisia on the German North Sea coast' In, van der Linden, W J M et al (eds) *Coastal Lowlands: Geology and Geotechnology* Kluwer, Dordrecht pp213–223

Streif, H 1990 'Quaternary sea-level changes in the North Sea: an analysis of amplitudes and velocities In, Brosche, P and Sundermann, J (eds) *Earth's Rotation from Eons to Days* Springer-Verlag, Berlin pp201–214

Tooley, M J 1971 'Changes in sea level and the implications for coastal development' *Association of River Authorities Yearbook and Directory* 1971 pp220–225

Tooley, M J 1974 'Sea-Level Changes during the last 9000 years in north-west England' *Geographical Journal* 140 pp18–42

Tooley, M J 1978 '*Sea-Level Changes: North-West England during The Flandrian Stage* Clarendon Press, Oxford

Tooley, M J 1982 'Sea-level changes in Northern England' *Proceedings of the Geological Association* 93 pp43–51

Tooley, M J 1989 'Global sea levels: floodwaters mark sudden rise' *Nature, London* 342 pp20–21

Turner, R K, Doktor, P and Adger, N 1994 'Assessing the economic costs of sea level rise' *Environment and Planning A* forthcoming

Walcott, R I 1972 'Past sea levels, eustasy and deformation of the Earth' *Quaternary Research* 2 pp1–14

Warrick, R A and Oerlemans, J 1990 'Sea-level rise' In, IPCC (Houghton, J T, Jenkins, G J and Ephraums, J J (eds)) *Climate Change: The IPCC Scientific Assessment* Cambridge University Press pp257–281

Wigley, T M L and Raper, S C B 1992 'Implications for climate and sea level of revised IPCC emissions scenarios' *Nature* 357 pp293–300

Zong, Y and Tooley, M J (in preparation) *Holocene sea-level changes and crustal movements in Morecambe Bay, North West England*

# Chapter 3 Implications for Water Supply and Water Management

Arnell, N W 1994 *Impact of Climate Change on Water Resources in the United Kingdom: Summary of Project Results* Report to Department of the Environment, Institute of Hydrology, Wallingford pp42

Arnell, N W and Reynard, N S 1993 *Impact of Climate Change on River Flow Regimes in the United Kingdom* Report to Department of the Environment Institute of Hydrology, Wallingford

Arnell, N W, Reynard, N S, Marsh, T J, Bryant, S J and Brown, R P C 1993 'Hydrology' In, Cannell, M G R and Pitcairn, C (eds) *Impacts of the Mild Winters and Hot Summers in the United Kingdom in 1988–1990* HMSO, London pp11–23

Arnell, N W, Jenkins, A and George, D G 1994 *The Implications of Climate Change for the National Rivers Authority* R & D Report 12 NRA, Bristol

Bate, R N and Dubourg, W R 1994 *A Net-back Analysis of Water Irrigation Demand in East Anglia* mimeo. Centre for Social and Economic Research on the Global Environment (CSERGE), University College London and University of East Anglia

CCIRG (Climatic Changes Impacts Review Group) 1991 *The Potential Effects of Climate Change in the United Kingdom* UK DoE Report Publication, HMSO

Coughlin, R E 1976 'The perception and valuation of water quality: a review of research method and findings' In, Craik, K H and Zube, E H (eds) *Perceiving Environmental Quality: Research and Applications* Plenum Press, New York

Dubourg, W R 1993 *The Sustainable Management of the Water Cycle: a Framework for Analysis* CSERGE paper WM 92-07, Centre for Social and Economic Research on the Global Environment (CSERGE), University College London and University of East Anglia

Dubourg, W R 1994a 'Water and water quality' In, Pearce, D W et al *Blueprint 3: Measuring Sustainable Development* Earthscan, London pp64–77

Dubourg, W R 1994b *The Sustainable Management of the Water Cycle: Economics and Policy* R & D Note 279, NRA, Bristol xvi + pp71

Dubourg, W R 1994c *Pricing for Sustainable Water Abstraction in England and Wales: a comparison of theory with practice* mimeo. Centre for Social and Economic Research on the Global Environment (CSERGE), University College London and University of East Anglia

Dubourg, W R and Pearce, D W 1994 'Paradigms for environmental choice: sustainability versus optimality' Presented at the AFCET/C3E symposium *Models of Sustainable Development: Exclusive or Complementary Approaches to Sustainability?*, Université Panthéon-Sorbonne, Paris, March

Hanley, N 1992 'Controlling water pollution using market mechanisms: results from empirical studies' In, Turner, R K (ed) *Sustainable Environmental Economics and Management: Principles and Practice* Belhaven, London pp360–382

Herrington, P 1990 *Notes on Sustainable Development and Resource Pricing for Water* OECD Workshop on Resource Pricing, May

Herrington, P and Hoschatt, M 1993 *Climate Change and the Demand for Water* Report to the Department of the Environment University of Leicester

Hewett, B A O, Harries, C D and Fenn, C R 1993 'Water resource planning in the uncertainty of climate change: a water company perspective' In, White, R (ed) *Engineering for Climate Change* Thomas Telford, London pp38–54

Jenkins, A, McCartney, M and Sefton, C 1993 *Impacts of Climate Change on River Water Quality in the United Kingdom* Report to Department of the Environment, Institute of Hydrology, Wallingford

Kelman, S 1981 *What Price Incentives – Economists and the Environment* Auburn House, Boston

Kneese, A V and Schulze, W D 1985 'Ethics and the environment' In, Kneese, A V and Sweeney, J L (eds) *Handbook of Natural Resource and Energy Economics* vol 1 Elsevier, Amsterdam

NRA 1991a *Demands and Resources of Water Undertakers in England and Wales* NRA, Bristol p40

NRA 1991b *The Quality of Rivers, Canals and Estuaries in England and Wales* NRA, Bristol

NRA 1991c *Water Resource Planning – Strategic Options* R & D Note 35 NRA, Bristol

NRA 1992 *Water Resources Development Strategy: a Discussion Document* NRA, Bristol

NRA 1993 *Scheme of Abstraction Charges 1993/94* NRA, Bristol

NRA 1994 *Water: Nature's Precious Resource: An Environmentally Sustainable Water Resources Development Strategy for England and Wales* NRA, Bristol

OFWAT 1991 *Report of the Director General of Water Services* OFWAT, Birmingham

Parker, D J, Green, C H and Thompson, P M 1987 *Urban Flood Protection Benefits: a Project Appraisal Guide* Gower, Aldershot

Pearce, D W et al 1994 *Blueprint 3: Measuring Sustainable Development* Earthscan, London

Trigg, A B and Dubourg, W R 1993 Valuing the environmental costs of opencast coal-mining: the case of the Trent Valley in North Staffordshire *Energy Policy* pp1110–1122

Welsh Water 1985 *Working Group Report on Welsh Salmon and Sea Trout Fisheries* Welsh Water, Brecon

Water Services Association 1993 *Waterfacts 1993* Water Services Association, London

# Chapter 4 Implications for Agriculture and Land Use

Baker, D, Doyle, C and Lidgate, H 1991 'Grass production' In, Thomas, C, Reeve, A and Fisher, G E J (eds) *Milk from Grass* 2nd edition, British Grassland Society, University of Reading

Brignall, A P and Rounsevell, M D A 1994 *The Effects of Future Climate Change on Crop Potential and Soil Tillage Opportunities in England and Wales* Environmental Change Unit, University of Oxford and Soil and Survey Land Research Centre, Cranfield University

Brouwer, F 1989 'Determination of broad scale land use changes by climate and soils' *Journal of Environmental Management* 29(1) pp1–15

Browning, G and Miller, J M 1992 'The association of year to year variation in average yield of pear cv. Conference in England with weather variables' *Journal of Horticultural Science* 67(5) pp593–599

Carter, T R, Parry, M L and Porter, J H 1991a 'Climatic change and future agroclimatic potential in Europe' *International Journal of Climatology* 11 pp251–269

Carter, T R, Porter, J H and Parry, M L 1991b 'Climatic warming and crop potential in Europe: prospects and uncertainties' *Global Environmental Change* 1(4) pp291–312

Davies, A, Shao, J, Bardgett, R D, Brignall, A P, Parry, M L and Pollock, C J 1994 *Specification of Climatic Sensitivity for UK Farming Systems* MAFF technical report

Dowle, K and Armstrong, A C 1990 'A Model for investment appraisal of grassland drainage schemes on farms in the UK' *Agriculture Water Management* 18 pp101–120

Hansen, J, Fung, I, Lacis, A, Rind, D, Lebedeff, S, Ruedy, R and Russell, G 1988 'Global climate changes as forecast by Goddard Institute for Space Studies Three-Dimensional Model' *Journal of Geophysical Research* 93 (D8) pp9341–9364

Harvey, D R, Rehman, T, Jones, P and Upton, M 1992 *The Centre for Agricultural Strategy Land Use Model* Paper presented at the Agricultural Economics Society Annual Conference, Aberdeen, April 1992

Hossell, J E, Jones, P J, Tehman, T, Tranter, R B, Marsh, J S, Parry, M L and Tayler, J C 1994 *Potential Effects of Climate Change on Agricultural Land Use and Production in England and Wales, and Implications for National Policy* Final report to the ESRC

Kvifte, G 1987 'Crop production and growth model for cereals, rape and grass at Aas, Norway' *Acta Agriculturae Scandinavica* 37 pp137–158

MacKerron, D K L and Waister, P D 1985 'A simple model of potato growth and yield. Part I. Model development and sensitivity analysis' *Agricultural and Forestry Meteorology* 34 pp241–252

Muchow, R C, Sinclair, T R and, Bennett, J M 1990 'Temperature and solar radiation effects on potential maize yield across locations' *Agronomy Journal* 82 pp338–343

Parry, M L, Hossell, J E, Jones, P J, Hehman, T, Tranter, R B, Marsh, J J and Carson, I G 'Integrating global and regional analysis of the effects of climate change: A case study of land use in England and Wales' *Climate Change* (in press)

Phipps, R H and Pain, B F 1978 'The efficiency of energy use in forage maize production' In, Bunting, E S (ed) *Forage Maize* Agricultural Research Council

Rosenzweig, C and Parry, M L 1994 'Potential effect of climate change on world food supply' *Nature* 367 pp133–138

Rounsevell, M D A and Brignall, A P 1994 'The potential effects of climate change on autumn soil tillage opportunities in England and Wales' *Soil and Tillage Research* (in press)

Rounsevell, M D A and Jones, R J A 1993 'A soil and agroclimatic model for estimating machinery work days: the basic model and climatic sensitivity' *Soil and Tillage Research* 26 pp179–191

Rowntree, P R 1990 'Estimates of future climatic change over Britain. Part 2: Results' *Weather* 45 (3) pp79–89

Thomasson, A J and Jones, R J A 1992 'An empirical approach to crop modelling and the assessment of land productivity' *Agricultural Systems* 37 pp351–367

# Chapter 5 Implications for Energy

British Gas plc 1992 *Financial and Operating Statistics for the Year Ended 31 December 1991* London

Cavallo, A J, Hock, S M and Smith, D R 1993 'Wind energy: technology and economics' In, Johansson, T B, Kelly, H, Reddy, A K N and Williams, R H (eds) *Renewable Energy: Source for Fuels and Energy* Island Press, Washington DC

CCIRG (Climatic Changes Impacts Review Group) 1991 *The Potential Effects of Climate Change in the United Kingdom* UK Department of the Environment Report Publication, HMSO

Chester, P 1988 'The potential for electricity from renewable energy sources' *Proceedings of the National Society for Clean Air 55th Annual Conference* Llandudno, October

Darmstadter, J 1991 *Processes for Identifying Regional Influences of and Responses to Increasing Atmospheric $CO_2$ and Climate Change – The MINK Project: Report V – Energy* DOE/RL/01830T-H, US Department of Energy, Washington DC, August

Department of Energy 1989 'The demand for energy' In, Helm D, Kay, J and Thompson, D *The Market for Energy* Clarendon Press, Oxford

Department of the Environment 1994 *Climate Change: The UK Programme* Cm 2427, HMSO, London, January 1994

Department of Trade and Industry 1992 *Energy Related Carbon Emissions in Future Scenarios for the UK* Energy Paper 59, HMSO, London, October

Department of Trade and Industry 1993a *Development of the Oil and Gas Resources of the United Kingdom* HMSO, London

Department of Trade and Industry 1993b *Digest of UK Energy Statistics 1993* HMSO, London

Department of Trade and Industry 1994 *New and Renewable Energy: Future Prospects in the UK* Energy Paper 62, HMSO, London, March 1994

Electricity Council 1988 *Annual Report and Accounts 1987/88* London

Eunson, E M 1988 *Proof of Evidence on System Considerations* Hinkley Point 'C' Power Station Public Inquiry, CEGB, London, September 1988

Fajer, E D and Bassaz, F A 1992 'Is carbon dioxide a good greenhouse gas? Effects of increasing carbon dioxide on ecological systems' *Global Environmental Change* pp301–310, December 1992

Grubb, M J and Meyer, N I 1993 'Wind energy: resources, systems and regional strategies' In, Johansson, T B et al (eds) *Renewable Energy: Source for Fuels and Energy* Island Press, Washington DC

Hardcastle, R 1984 *The Pattern of Energy Use in the UK* Energy Efficiency Series 2, Energy Efficiency Office, HMSO, London, April 1984

Herring, H, Hardcastle, R and Philipson, R 1988 *Energy Use and Energy Efficiency in UK Commercial and Public Buildings up to the Year 2000* Energy Efficiency Series 6, Energy Efficiency Office, HMSO, London

Hillsman, E L and Petrich, C H 1994 *Potential Vulnerability of Renewable Energy Systems to Climate Change* Report ORNL-6802, Oak Ridge National Laboratory, Oak Ridge, Tennessee

IPCC 1990 *Climate Change: The IPCC Impacts Assessment* Australian Government Publishing Service, Canberra

McGillivray, D G, Agnew, T A, McKay, G A, Pilkington, G R and Hill, M C 1993 *Impacts of Climate Change on the Beaufort Sea-Ice Regime: Implications for the Arctic Petroleum Industry* CCD 93-01, Environment Canada, Downsview, Ontario

Milbank, N 1989 'Building design and use: response to climate change' *Architects Journal* 96 pp59–63

Miller, B A, Alavian, V, Bender, M D, Benton, D J, Ostrowski, P, Parsly, J A, Samples, H M and Shiao, M C 1992 *Impact of Incremental Changes in Meteorology on Thermal Compliance and Power System Operations* Report WR28-1-680-109, Tennessee Valley Authority Engineering Laboratory, Norris, Tennessee, February 1992

National Academy of Sciences 1992 *Policy Implications of Greenhouse Warming: Mitigation, Adaptation and the Science Base* National Academy Press, Washington DC

NGC Settlement Systems 1993, 1994 *Pool Price Data* Birmingham

Parry, M L and Read, N J 1988 *The Impact of Climatic Variability on UK Industry* AIR Report 1, Atmospheric Impacts Research Group, University of Birmingham

Sakai, S 1988 *The Impact of Climate Variation on Secondary and Tertiary Industry in Japan* Meteorological Note 180, pp163–173 (Japanese language)

Wolock, D M, McCabe, G J, Tasker, G D, Ayers, M A and Hay, L E 1992 'Sensitivity of water resources in the Delaware River basin to climate' *Proceedings of the Workshop on the Effects of Global Climate Change on Hydrology and Water Resources at the Catchment Scale* Tsukuba, Japan, 3–6 February

World Energy Council 1993 *Energy for Tomorrow's World* Kogan Page/St Martin's Press, London

# Chapter 6 Implications for Insurance and Finance

Anderson, J and Black, A 1993 'Tay flooding' *Circulation Newsletter of the British Hydrological Society* 38 May

Boer, G J, McFarlane, N A and Lazare, M 1992 'Greenhouse gas-induced climate change simulated with the CCC second-generation general circulation model' *Journal of Climate* 5 pp1045–1077

Broccoli, A J, and Manabe S 1990 'Can existing climate models be used to study anthropogenic changes in tropical cyclone climate?' *Geophysical Research Letters* 17 pp1917–1920

Buller, P S J 1988 *The October Gale of 1987* Building Research Establishment, Department of the Environment

Cohen, S J 1990 'Bringing the global warming issue closer to home: the challenge of regional impact studies' *Bulletin of the American Meteorological Society* 71 pp520–526

Dlugolecki, A 1991 'Financial sector' In, Parry, M (ed) *Potential Effects of Climate Change in the United Kingdom* Department of Environment, HMSO

Dlugolecki, A, Clement, D, Elvy, C, Kirby, G, Palutikof, J, Salthouse, R, Toomer, C, Turner, S and Witt, D 1994 *The Impact of Changing Weather Patterns on*

*Property Insurance* Chartered Insurance Institute, London

Doornkamp, J C 1993 'Clay shrinkage induced subsidence' *Geographical Journal* 159 (2) 196–202

Gates, W L, Mitchell, J F B, Boer, G J, Cubash, U and Meleshko, V P 1992 'Climate modelling, climate prediction and model validation' In, IPCC (Houghton, J T, Callander, B A, and Varney, S K (eds)) *Climate Change 1992: The Supplementary Report to the IPCC Scientific Assessment* Cambridge University Press pp97–134

Giorgi, F and Mearns, L O 1991 'Approaches to the simulation of regional climate change: a review' *Reviews of Geophysics* 29 pp191–216

Glantz, M H, Katz, R W and Nicolls, N (eds) 1991 *Teleconnections: Linking Worldwide Climate Anomalies* Cambridge University Press

Gordon, H B, Whetton, P H, Fowler, A M and Haylock, M R 1992 'Simulated changes in daily rainfall intensity due to the enhanced greenhouse effect: implications for extreme rainfall events' *Climate Dynamics* 8 pp83–102

Greenpeace International 1994 *The Climate Time Bomb* Stichting Greenpeace Council, Amsterdam

Gregory, J M 1993 'Sea level change under increasing atmospheric $CO_2$ in a transient coupled ocean–atmosphere GCM experiment' *Journal of Climate* 6 pp2247–2262

Gregory, J M, Wigley, T M L and Jones, P D 1993 'Application of Markov models to area–average daily precipitation series and interannual variability in seasonal totals' *Climate Dynamics* 8 pp299–310

Grotch, S L and MacCraken, M C 1991 'The use of general circulation models to predict regional climate change', *Journal of Climate* 4, pp286–303

Haarsma, R J, Mitchell, J F B and Senior, C A 1993 'Tropical disturbances in a GCM' *Climate Dynamics* 8 pp247–257

Hall, N M J, Hoskins, B J, Valdes, P J and Senior, C A 1994 'Storm tracks in a high resolution GCM with doubled $CO_2$' *Quarterly Journal of the Royal Meteorological Society* (in press)

Hammond, J M 1990 'The strong winds experienced during the late winter of 1989/1990 over the United Kingdom: historical perspectives' *Meteorological Magazine* 119 pp211–219

Hansen, J, Lacis, A, Rind, D, Russell, L, Stone, P, Fung, I, Ruedy, R and Lerner, J 1984 'Climate sensitivity analysis of feedback mechanisms' In, Hansen, J and Takahashi, T (eds) *Climate Processes and Climate Sensitivity* Geophysical Monograph 29 Washington DC American Geophysical Union, pp130–160

Hansen, J, Rind, D, Russell, L, Stone, P, Fung, I, Ruedy, R and Lerner, J 1989 'Climate sensitivity analysis of feedback mechanisms' In, Hansen, J, and Takahashi, T (eds) *Climate Processes and Climate Sensitivity* Geophysical Monograph 29 Washington DC American Geophysical Union, pp130–163

Hulme, M and Jones, P D 1991 'Temperatures and windiness over the UK during the winters of 1988/89 and 1989/90 compared with previous years' *Weather* 46 pp126–135

IPCC (Houghton, J T, Callander, B A, and Varney, S K (eds)) 1992 *Climate Change 1992: The Supplementary Report to the IPCC Scientific Assessment* Cambridge University Press

Jenkinson, A F and Collison, F P 1977 'An initial climatology of gales over the North Sea' *Synoptic Climatology Branch Memorandum No. 62* UK Meteorological Office, Bracknell p18

Jones, P D and Briffa, K R 1992 'Global surface air temperature variations during the twentieth century: Part I, spatial, temporal and seasonal details' *The Holocene* 2 pp165–179

Katz, R W and Brown, B B 1992 'Extreme events in a changing climate: variability is more important than averages' *Climatic Change* 21 pp289–302

Manabe, S and Wetherald, R T 1987 'Large scale changes of soil wetness induced by an increase in atmospheric carbon dioxide' *Journal of Atmospheric Science* 44 pp1211–1235

Mearns, L O, Katz, R and Schneider, S H 1984 'Extreme high-temperature events: changes in their probabilities with changes in mean temperature' *Journal of Climate and Applied Meteorology* 23 pp1601–1613

Mitchell, J F B, Manabe, S, Meleshko, V and Tokioka, T 1990 'Equilibrium climate change – and its implications for the future' In, IPCC (Houghton, J T, Jenkins, G J, and Ephraums, J J (eds)) *Climate Change: The IPCC Scientific Assessment* Cambridge University Press pp131–172

Mullan, A B and Renwick, J A 1990 *Climate Change in the New Zealand Region Inferred from General Circulation Models* New Zealand Meteorological Service, Wellington pp142

Muth, M 1993 'Facing up to the losses' *The McKinsey Quarterly* 2

Noda, A and Tokioka, T 1989 'The effect of doubling the $CO_2$ concentration on convective and non-convective precipitation in a general circulation model coupled with a simple mixed-layer ocean' *Journal of the Meteorological Society of Japan* 67 pp1055–1067

Palutikof, J P, Goodess, G M and Guo, X 1994 'Climate change, potential evapotranspiration and moisture availability in the Mediterranean Basin' *International Journal of Climatology* (in press)

Palutikof, J P, Guo, X, Wigley, T M L and Gregory, J M 1992 'Regional changes in climate in the Mediterranean Basin due to global greenhouse warming' *MAP Technical Report Series 66* Mediterranean Action Plan, United Nations Environment Programme, Athens pp172

Parry, M L 1978 *Climate Change, Agriculture and Settlement* Dawson, Folkstone

Racsko, P, Szeidl, L and Semenov, M 1991 'A serial approach to local stochastic weather models' *Ecological Modelling* 57 pp27–41

Rind, D, Goldberg, R, Hansen, J, Rosenzweig, C and Ruedy, R 1990 'Potential evapotranspiration and the likelihood of future drought' *Journal of Geophysical Research* 95 pp9983–10004

Rosenzweig, C and Parry, M L 1994 'Potential impact of climate change on world food supply' *Nature* 367 pp133–138

Smith, S G 1982 'An index of windiness for the United Kingdom' *Meteorological Magazine* 111 pp232–247

Tol, R S J (ed) 1993 *Socio-Economic and Policy Aspects of Change in the Incidence and Intensity of Extreme Weather Events* Amsterdam Workshop 24–25 June, Free University of Amsterdam

Warrick, R A and Oerlemans, H 1990 'Sea-level rise' In, IPCC (Houghton, J T, Jenkins, G J and Ephraums, J J (eds)) *Climate Change: The IPCC Scientific Assessment* Cambridge University Press pp257–281

Wetherald, R T and Manabe, S 1986 'Cloud feedback processes in a general circulation model' *Journal of Atmospheric Sciences* 45 pp1397–1415

Whetton, P H, Fowler, A M, Haylock, M R and Pittock, A B 1993 Implications of climate change due to the enhanced greenhouse effect on floods and droughts in Australia *Climatic Change* 25 pp289–317

Wigley, T M L 1985 'Impact of extreme events' *Nature* 316 pp106–107

# Chapter 7 Greenhouse Policies and the Costs of Mitigation

Agarwal, A and Narain, S 1991 *Global Warming in an Unequal World: a Case of Environmental Colonialism* Centre for Science and Environment, New Delhi, India

Barker, T, Baylis, S and Madsen, P A 1993 'UK carbon/energy tax: the macroeconomic effects' *Energy Policy* 21 (3) pp296–308

Cline, W R 1992 *Optimal Carbon Emissions over Time: Experiments with the Nordhaus DICE Model* Mimeo. Institute for International Economics, Washington DC

Cline, W R 1994 'The costs and benefits of greenhouse abatement: a guide to policy analysis In, OECD *The Economics of Global Warming* Paris

Crosson, P R and Rosenberg, N J 1993 'An Overview of the MINK Study' *Climatic Change* 24 (1/2) pp159–173

Department of the Environment 1992 *Climate Change: Our National Programme for $CO_2$ Emissions* UK Department of the Environment

Easterling, W E III, Crosson, P R, Rosenberg, N J, McKenney, M S, Katz, L A and Lemon, K M 1993 'Agricultural impacts of and responses to climate change in the Missouri-Iowa-Nebraska-Kansas (MINK) region' *Climatic Change* 24 (1/2) pp23–62

Fankhauser, S 1994a *Valuing Climate Change. The Economics of the Greenhouse Effect* Earthscan, London

Fankhauser, S 1994b 'Protection versus retreat: the economic costs of sea level rise' *Environment and Planning* A forthcoming

Hope, C W, Anderson, J and Wenman, P 1993 'Policy analysis of the greenhouse effect' *Energy Policy* 21(3) pp327–338

IPCC (Houghton, J T, Jenkins, G J, and Ephraums, J J (eds)) 1990 *Climate Change: The IPCC Scientific Assessment* Cambridge University Press

Kalkstein, LS 1989 'The impact of $CO_2$ and trace gas-induced climate change upon human mortality' In, Smith, J B and Tirpak, D A (eds) *The Potential Effects of Global Climate Change on the United States. Appendix G: Health* US Environmental Protection Agency, Washington DC

Leggett, J 1991 'Energy and the new politics of the environment' *Energy Policy* 19(2) pp161–171

Manne, A S and Richels, R G 1991 'Buying greenhouse insurance' *Energy Policy* 19(6) pp543–552

Mendelsohn, R, Nordhaus, W D and Shaw, D 1992 *The Impact of Climate on*

*Agriculture: A Ricardian Approach* Cowles Foundation, Discussion Paper No 1010, New Haven, Connecticut

Nordhaus, W D 1993a 'Optimal greenhouse gas reductions and tax policy in the 'DICE' model' *American Economic Review, Papers and Proceedings* 83(2) pp313–317

Nordhaus, W D 1993b 'Rolling the 'DICE': an optimal transition path for controlling greenhouse gases' *Resources and Energy Economics* 15(1) pp27–50

Parry, M L 1990 *Climate Change and World Agriculture* Earthscan, London

Rosenzweig, C and Parry, M L 1994 'Potential effect of climate change on world food supply' *Nature* 367 pp133–138

Schelling, T 1992 'Some economics of global warming' *American Economic Review* 82(1) pp1–14

Smith, J B and Tirpak, D A (eds) 1989 *The Potential Effects of Global Climate Change on the United States* US Environmental Protection Agency, Washington DC

World Resources Institute 1992 *World Resources 1992–93. A Guide to the Global Environment* Oxford University Press, New York

# Index